HIGH COMMITMENT WORKPLACES

Stephen L. Fink

1992

Q

Quorum Books

New York • Westport, Connecticut • London

Library of Congress Cataloging-in-Publication Data

Fink, Stephen L.
    High commitment workplaces / Stephen L. Fink.
        p. cm.
        Includes bibliographical references (p.   ) and index.
        ISBN 0-89930-740-X (alk. paper)
        1. Job enrichment.   2. Job satisfaction.   3. Employee motivation.
    4. Quality of work life.   5. Commitment (Psychology).   I. Title.
    HF5549.5.J616F55 1992
    658.3'14—dc20   91-42768

British Library Cataloguing in Publication Data is available.

Library of Congress Catalog Card Number: 91-42768
ISBN: 0-89930-740-X

First published in 1992

Quorum Books, One Madison Avenue, New York, NY 10010
An imprint of Greenwood Publishing Group, Inc.

Printed in the United States of America

The paper used in this book complies with the
Permanent Paper Standard issued by the National
Information Standards Organization (Z39.48-1984).

10   9   8   7   6   5   4   3   2   1

Copyright Acknowledgment

W. N. Murray, *The Scottish Himalayan Expedition,* 1951, J. M. Dent & Sons,
Ltd., London, reprinted by permission.

Contents

Tables and Figures

Preface

I once was told that what people choose to study or write about always is a reflection of some inner personal struggle that has never been resolved. I am not sure that is always the case, but I do know that it has been true for me in writing this book. William Thurston, former Chief Executive Officer of Genrad Corporation, whom I interviewed in the early stages of writing the book, told me he felt that all commitment begins with commitment to oneself, to some personal mission in life. Without that, he said, one's life would be pointless. It is a pretty strong statement, but I believe it to be true. It gave me pause to think about my own mission in life and just what writing this book represented in that sense. What I concluded is that it represented putting myself on the line, saying what I wanted to say without equivocating about an idea that is important to me. Perhaps it is best reflected in this excerpt from W. N. Murray's *The Scottish Himalayan Expedition,* written in 1951:

> Until one is committed
> there is hesitancy, the chance to draw back,
> always ineffectiveness.
>
> Concerning all acts of initiative (and creation)
> there is one elementary truth,
> the ignorance of which kills countless ideas
> and splendid plans:
> that the moment one definitely commits oneself,
> then Providence moves too.
> All sorts of things occur to help one
> that would otherwise never have occurred.
> A whole stream of events issues from the decision,
> raising in one's favor all manner
> of unforeseen incidents and meetings
> and material assistance,
> which no man could have dreamt

would have come his way.
I have learned a deep respect
for one of Goethe's couplets:

'Whatever you can do, or dream you can . . . begin it.
Boldness has genius, power and magic in it.'

Acknowledgments

The beginnings of this book go back more than eight years. I cannot, therefore, even begin to remember all the various conversations I had with people who influenced my thinking. However, I do recall distinctly that the process began with a sabbatical year in 1983, when I planned to write a book on the use of humor in managing. I never quite got started on that project before I had a conversation with my friend and colleague, Allan Cohen, in which he happened to mention something about commitment being the key issue of the coming era in management. I thank Allan for planting the seed, which now has grown to maturity.

Over the years I had opportunities to discuss my work with other colleagues, including Maurice Olivier, whose responses always energized me, and all my close friends and partners in the Portsmouth Consulting Group, who had a major impact on the final formulation of the concepts presented in this book.

I owe a special expression of appreciation to Susan Herman, whose willingness to join forces in the research part of my work enabled me to move the project along at a much faster pace than otherwise might have been possible. Susan's own work on organizational spirit served as an excellent complement to mine. I hope to see her work receive its deserved recognition some day.

I certainly want to thank the Whittemore School of Business and Economics at the University of New Hampshire for supporting my research over the years, especially for allowing me to occupy office space during the sabbatical year when I wrote the book. Dean Lyndon Goodridge never raised any question about this arrangement; for this I owe him a vote of thanks. Wayne Burton was kind enough to provide whatever limited funds were available to pay for graduate students' assistance in conducting the research. Kim Miller turned out to be a major source of help.

Then there was Carol True, who must have typed a hundred versions and variations of the research instrument without ever showing any sign of exasperation with the job. Carol has been my anchor in a rather chaotic environment; I thank her for that.

The one colleague I cannot thank enough is Peter Royce, who became my statistical and computer consultant throughout the period of the research. He never failed to come to my rescue when I was in trouble with my data, and he was willing to sit for hours working with the data and exploring the best methods of analysis. I know he learned a great deal from the collaboration, but he definitely gave me more than I ever could have expected in time and commitment.

In some ways the person to whom I owe the most for the completion of this project is John Harney, whose instinctive faith in my ability to complete the work inspired me more than anything else. He made his initial judgment based on a conversation in my office, without the usual formalities of a proposal, an outline, sample chapters, a market analysis, and all the usual support data that a publisher normally requires before making an offer. As the project moved along, John and I did discover a few areas of difference when it came to writing style and with respect to some of the ways in which I had organized the book. We argued some of these points, and I did make some major changes based on his suggestions. I also held to some of my own preferences, which John graciously supported, but I always found his comments thoughtful and worthy of careful consideration. I believe the book is all the better for his participation.

The one person who deserves a medal for tolerance is Elaine, my wife of thirty-six years. I am a person who drifts off in thought even when I am not working on anything especially absorbing. But combine that tendency with an obsession and I become a genuine "space cadet." I know she will be happy when I return to Earth, but her patience until I do is appreciated beyond expression. To her I dedicate this book.

HIGH COMMITMENT
WORKPLACES

Chapter 1

The Importance of Commitment

Three Cases: Linda, Gary, and Anne

Linda works in the information systems division of a large insurance company. She works long hours, but often does not even realize it. Sometimes she can be found at her computer on weekends and evenings. She describes her work as fun and says that sometimes she loses all sense of time when she is solving a challenging problem. Linda's supervisor says that he never has to worry about her hours or whether she will get her work finished. He wishes he had more employees like Linda.

Gary is part of a production team at a company that manufactures instrument panels for the major automobile companies. The team has been together for over a year, works hard to maintain its level of productivity and quality standards, and always is ready to put forth extra effort when needed. Gary says that what he really likes about the job is the "feeling of family" that exists in the team. The work itself, he says, is not terrific and can get to be a little monotonous, but he also says that he tries not to miss any work time because it might hang up the team.

Anne is a dietary worker in a large urban hospital. She works the early morning shift, which prepares the breakfasts for patients, many of whom are aged and seriously ill. Anne usually works by herself, preparing trays for delivery to the patients' rooms; the work varies little from day to day. But Anne is there every day and has been doing her job for more than twenty years. When asked why she has been so reliable and dedicated, Anne always has the same answer: "These are sick people and it's my job to help them feel better and maybe get better. The hospital counts on me and I can't let it down."

Linda, Gary, and Anne all are committed to their jobs, but for very different reasons. In all three cases the work gets done, they can be depended upon to be at their jobs, and each might be considered an ideal employee. However, understanding the differences in the reasons for their commitment is just as important as simply identifying them as highly committed. Linda strongly identifies with the work that she does; she sees it as a part of herself and often becomes totally absorbed in it. This is not the case for Gary or Anne. Gary identifies with the team. He would never permit himself to let it down. Anne believes in the hospital and what it does for people; contributing to that effort is what drives her behavior. Again, all three show high levels of commitment, but for very different reasons. It is those reasons that are the subject of this book.

Background

About eight years ago I began to informally interview managers about their views on commitment. I also used sessions in executive development programs as opportunities to discuss various meanings of the concept. The interviews and the discussions produced similar results. Some people defined commitment relative to the organization. In fact, most upper level managers defined it that way. Others, usually middle and lower level managers, defined it more in relation to groups, including departments and work teams. Only a few saw commitment in terms of the work itself, removed from the context of a department or organization. It was not until I spent some time talking to employees, both professional and technical, that I heard frequent reference to work.

A few senior executives seemed to have perspectives that did encompass more than just commitment to the organization and included identification with work and co-workers. For example, William Thurston, former president of Genrad Corporation, told me, "The company is the people and the working relationships. A working relationship consists mostly of requests, promises, commitments, and fulfillments. The company is most importantly a dynamic web of commitments each of us has made to others . . . to people outside as well as inside." Gary Countryman, president of Liberty Mutual Insurance Company, showed his awareness of the connection betweeen visionary leadership and the empowerment of the individual employee when he stated, "I try to create a vision of where we want to go in the future, but I try to connect that vision to the past, so that the future is a natural extension of the past." With respect to the lower levels of the organization, Countryman added, "We need to give them the chance to do their thing without controlling them so much that we discourage entrepreneurship and risk-taking. I would rather rein them in than have to herd them along."

A search of the literature, academic and popular, revealed a fairly one-sided picture. I found almost all definitions of commitment pertained to the organization as a whole; very few definitions included the work or relationships as independent dimensions. In some cases there was reference to job involvement as a variable separate from commitment (Blau and Boal, 1987), but not as a means of *generating* commitment.

There is nothing inherently wrong with defining and studying commitment as a unidimensional variable related to an organization as a whole. However, it is a limited perspective that fails to reveal some of the important dynamics offered by a multidimensional view. For example, the three dimensions suggested earlier would generate very different commitment profiles for Linda, Gary, and Anne. Each profile would suggest a different set of actions, or interventions, to enhance commitment in all three areas for these three individuals.

In Linda's case, it might be important over the long run to help her see the connections between her work and that of others in the department, as well as to the company's overall goals. In Gary's situation, it could become necessary to redesign the way the work is carried out, in order to make it more challenging and to help him to see how his efforts contribute to organizational objectives. And in Anne's case it would seem useful for management to restructure her work to make it less isolated and more varied. Efforts like these can go a long way toward building and sustaining employee commitment.

Today's Employees: Commitment versus Compliance

Employee commitment will become increasingly important in the coming decade because more and more companies are moving the decision-making processes farther down the organizational hierarchy, making it almost impossible for management to control performance directly. Incentives and sanctions can go a long way to sustain performance, but what better situation can managers have than one in which they are confident in employees' own desire to do their best for the sake of the department and the system as a whole? As the use of self-managing work teams increases, it will be incumbent on managers to find ways to enhance employees' identification with their work, their teams, and the company.

Furthermore, as the educational levels of employees increase (and they are increasing), the demand for greater challenge, variety, and responsibility in a job also will increase. Blocked opportunities for career advancement and personal development will not be offset by increased financial rewards. As we have learned many times over, money can serve as a temporary boost to performance, but rarely does it have a long-term, self-sustaining impact; it certainly does not change one's degree of identification with the organization.

Interestingly enough, some of the more recent literature on leadership does reflect at least an implicit recognition of employee commitment in a multidimensional sense. For example, the concepts of developmental leadership and transformational leadership (both of which are discussed in Chapter 3) emphasize the importance of employee empowerment, team building, and overall company vision-sharing. These approaches all recognize the importance of commitment, as opposed to compliance, as the most effective route to productivity.

The so-called transactional manager, who views things in terms of a simple exchange of pay for work, seeks employee loyalty as part of the bargain. Whether that loyalty truly represents commitment (as opposed to "honoring the deal") is hard to tell, but genuine commitment usually has a life of its own and is sustained even in hard times when the so-called bargain cannot be fully honored. In fact, company loyalty may go up or down depending upon the manner in which management treats its employees.

Although Japanese companies are known for their ability to solicit employee loyalty in exchange for lifetime employment, a recent survey of one thousand senior employees of major companies in Japan revealed that over 70 percent said they would rather work elsewhere (*Wall Street Journal,* April 23, 1991). Evidently, genuine commitment to the organization was lacking among the employees surveyed. A study by Luthans, McCaul, and Dodd in 1985 compared Japanese, Korean, and American employees in terms of organizational commitment. Their results showed that the American workers were significantly more committed to their organizations than were either the Japanese or Korean workers.

Company commitment—identification with the mission or purposes of the organization—can sustain itself despite shifts in managerial practices, unless those practices undermine the essential character of the organization and what it represents. Certainly a radical change at the top can rapidly erode whatever sense of organizational identification has developed over the years, but such a change would have to go deeper than one that simply changed the ground rules for employees.

How This Book Will Help Managers

For the manager who wishes to understand and strengthen employee commitment, this book will:

1. Identify signs that indicate a problem with employee commitment;
2. Determine the specific nature or source of the problem: whether it is related to the work itself, the relationships among employees, and/or the overall organization;
3. Demonstrate a way to measure, by means of a reliable and valid instrument as well as by less formal methods, the levels of commitment in each of the three areas—work, co-workers, and organization;
4. Determine potential strategies and methods for addressing specific problems;
5. Develop organizational, group, and/or individual profiles of commitment, as well as a means of assessing the impact of any intervention;
6. Outline and discuss specific managerial actions that can help to build individual, group, and organizational commitment;
7. Offer suggestions for dealing with a number of difficult problems faced by managers today.

In general, this book will provide managers with a diagnostic framework for understanding and managing employee commitment. It will not offer any quick solutions to serious problems, but it will help managers sort out relevant information and formulate approaches that have high potential for solving problems.

Augmenting the Literature

In their review of commitment research, Steers and Porter (1983) describe a very mixed picture in which it remains uncertain just how levels of employee commitment affect and are affected by important organizational variables, such as performance, turnover, tenure, and absenteeism. Cause and effect relationships remain unclear, as do the effects of other moderating variables, such as ability, role clarity, and expectations. In this book, I expect to add some clarity by showing how various elements tend to relate more to one dimension of commitment or another and not necessarily to all three. In other words, in treating commitment in strictly organizational terms, previous research has been only partially successful in establishing empirical links between measures of commitment and other factors. As will be shown, some relationships tend to exist for commitment to the work itself, and not for commitment to co-workers or the organization. The importance of this kind of distinction, as illustrated in the three examples described earlier, cannot be overstated, especially when managers are seeking ways to build and enhance the levels of commitment of their employees.

One of the interesting issues that emerged in the research for this book is related to an apparent contradiction in the behavior and attitudes of many of the managers who provided data. This contradiction was not only evident in the data itself, but also in their behavior and attitudes while discussing what the data showed. The contradiction pertained directly to the notion of teamwork.

Although most managers were emphatically in favor of teamwork, their language reflected a highly competitive attitude, even in relation to their peers. For them, teamwork among their employees clearly was important, but their own actions in relation to their peers tended to contradict what they espoused. This was evident to many of their own employees, as reflected in their written comments. On several occasions I pointed this out and usually received the same response: "We get rewarded for individual effort, not group effort." This struck me as a key problem in promoting employee commitment to a team effort. While it was no surprise, the importance of the problem was strongly reinforced by the data.

As will be shown, the results of my research do establish a clear relationship between commitment and performance. More than that, it also sheds some light on why previous studies found what has been described as only a weak relationship between commitment and performance.

Format

This book is divided into three main sections. This chapter and Chapters 2 and 3 set the stage conceptually. Chapter 2 presents the overall framework for understanding the role of employee commitment within the larger context of organizational variables; Chapter 3 provides some historical background for the three dimensions of commitment, as well as a brief review of research on the topic.

The second section of the book covers the research that establishes an empirical basis for understanding the importance of employee commitment to the achievement of organizational goals. Chapter 4 describes the development of the Commitment Diagnosis Instrument (CDI), the pilot study used to refine it, and the design of the research conducted at two organizations. Chapter 5 reports the results and Chapter 6 discusses the theoretical and practical implications of the findings. Chapter 7 shows how the CDI can be used in an action-research approach to organizational development, both formally and informally.

The third part of the book is devoted to managerial applications of commitment as three dimensional. Chapter 8 presents eight profiles that represent different combinations of highs and lows in the three dimensions, how these profiles are manifested in actual behavior, and just how a manager might use them to diagnose and change undesirable patterns of employee behavior. Chapter 9 offers practical suggestions for building employee commitment to the work itself; Chapter 10 discusses methods of building co-worker and team identification; and Chapter 11 covers systemwide interventions that can foster total organizational commitment. Chapter 12 is concerned with a number of critical issues that organizations today are encountering, issues that can have a major impact on an organization's ability to sustain employee commitment over the long term.

I want to point out to those who do not have a research bent and, therefore, might shy away from quantitative data and statistical analysis, that Appendix B provides a brief introduction to statistical methods designed to make reading and understanding Chapter 5 quite easy. For many readers this introduction may be totally unnecessary, but I wanted to make sure that people who either lacked the necessary background, or forgot much of what they had once learned, did not just skip this part of the book.

Chapter 2

How to Think about Commitment

An organization is a dynamic, living system. Employee commitment is only one of many factors that affect performance, but it certainly is a key factor. Therefore, we will look at the meaning of employee commitment within the larger context of the organization.

Commitment: A Three-dimensional Concept

Commitment is an attitude that develops from a process called *identification,* which occurs when one experiences something, someone, or some idea as an extension of oneself.

As indicated in Chapter 1, almost all research on commitment treats it in terms of identification with the organization, that is, its goals, values, and mission. Little attention has been given to ways in which employees identify with their *work* or their *co-workers*. These are equally important because we know that they can have powerful effects upon employee performance.

An important advantage of a multidimensional view of commitment is that it allows a manager to develop a diagnostic profile that leads to interventions close to the heart of a problem. The examples of Linda, Gary, and Anne demonstrate this point. Knowing whether employees are committed is less useful than being able to pinpoint what they are committed to.

What is offered here is a method of developing that profile. A profile shows by pattern the relative levels of commitment in the three categories for an individual, a group, or even the organization as a whole. These profiles have important diagnostic value, since they help managers develop focused solutions to problems. Chapter 8 presents eight basic profiles frequently found in today's organizations. Many, if not all, will be familiar to experienced managers.

Figure 2.1. Conceptual Framework

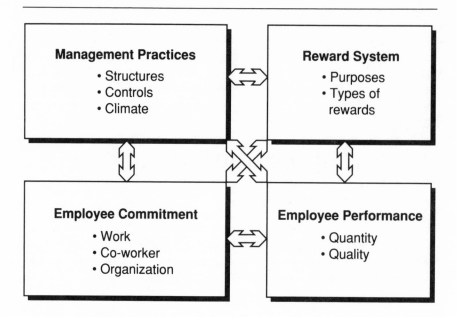

A Conceptual Framework

In addition to their levels of commitment, employees are affected by an organization's reward system, its performance appraisal process, its general management practices, and its culture. The organization's culture is the myriad of norms, customs, and behavior patterns that have emerged over its history. Figure 2.1 is a conceptual framework that shows where commitment fits into the constellation of organizational forces. Note that the framework is interactive, not linear.

For our purposes, *management practices* refers to the overall style or ways in which the organization manages itself, focusing on three features: the way in which the organization has structured itself and its work; the ways in which the organization exercises control over its activities and its employees; and the overall climate that management creates in the organization. These three factors were chosen because they provide important and specific connections to employee commitment.

In the area of reward systems, which have a very powerful impact upon both commitment and performance, the emphasis will be on two factors: the different purposes served by rewards and the different kinds of rewards that serve those purposes. The matching of rewards to purposes is a critical process in the generation of employee commitment. As will be shown, this is not simple because some consequences of that matching include inherent conflicts between long-term and short-term effects.

The bottom line is employee performance, both quantity and quality. It is assumed that: 1) employee performance is affected by many factors, including management practices, the reward system, and the employees' own levels of commitment to the job, co-workers, and the organization; 2) the performance levels of employees have an impact, both directly and indirectly, on management practices and on the rewards dispensed by the organization; and 3) an individual's performance provides a kind of feedback that can either enhance or diminish that person's level of commitment in any one or more of the three categories.

In summary, we are looking at a dynamic, interactive model that suggests the following connections:

1. Good management practices result in
   a. an effective reward system and
   b. employee commitment

2. An effective reward system results in enhanced
   a. employee commitment and
   b. employee performance

3. Employee commitment results in enhanced employee performance.

The model depicts these relationships as reciprocal, not linear or one-way. It shows how employee performance (the principal outcome) is affected by several factors and affects those factors in return.

Now let us look at each part of the framework in greater detail.

Management Practices

Organizational Structure. Modern organizations have moved far beyond the constraints of traditional hierarchy or chain of command. With the explosion in information technology, the demands for rapid response and turnaround times in manufacturing and service industries, the need for flexibility in dealing with unpredictable and turbulent changes in the market, and the necessity for decisions to be made close to the scene of action, most organizations have found that working through channels simply does not work. It fails to give a company the competitive edge it needs, and it fails to make the best use of its resources, both technical and human.

This is not to say that any form of hierarchy is obsolete or dysfunctional. That is hardly the case. Each level of an organization represents a different perspective, from specific to general, as one goes up the system. Those different perspectives provide the integration that keeps the organization focused on common goals. The chain-of-command model becomes dysfunctional when it impedes the flow of information needed to make decisions and when organizational politics become the principal factor that determines the flow of that information.

Galbraith (1973) presented a way of thinking about alternative organizational structures in terms of the reduction of *uncertainty*. He defined *uncertainty* as the gap between information needed to make a decision and information available to the decision-maker when needed. His main thesis was that the more traditional organizational forms impede information flow and thereby increase the level of uncertainty in decision-making. The alternative forms Galbraith discussed were essentially generic ways of thinking about organizational structures rather than specific forms. He offered the idea of *self-contained units,* which possessed all the necessary resources to manage any given situation; he discussed the use of computer technology as a way of moving information rapidly to scenes of action; he looked at the use of slack resources that would always be available for unanticipated demands; and he gave special attention to the use of lateral relationships that cut across traditional channels as a highly flexible and responsive means of reducing decision-making uncertainty.

Whatever recent changes and innovations we have observed in organizational structuring have used Galbraith's concepts in one way or another. We do not even need to discuss the use of computers; few organizations today could survive without them. What is especially significant about the advances in information technology is that they are driving more and more organizations away from traditional models and into more open and flexible systems.

For awhile it looked as though the matrix organization was the ultimate form; then the strategic business unit emerged as the form most responsive to specific markets. Many organizations combine the two models, creating highly flexible and responsive small organizations within larger corporations.

The next generation of organizational structures undoubtedly will capitalize on the major advances in information technology and will look more like sets of interconnected networks of people, material, and financial resources, all working to accomplish common, interdependent objectives. Gareth Morgan describes the change as a shift from "discrete organization with identifiable boundaries" to "more amorphous networks" in which "interdependence is the key" (1988, p. 129). In the network the role of management is one of integrator, managing the connections among the various groupings and making sure that the parts work cohesively. But the transition from hierarchy to networks is far from easy for most employees. The chief executive officer of a major insurance company told me in an interview:

If you break up the existing structures, some people will lose their departmental identities, so you have to be sure you replace the structures with new sources of identity for people . . . new product lines, or activities that are meaningful.

He also mentioned the importance of people not just "doing their own thing," emphasizing that "by seeing the wider array of opportunities in the company as a whole, they are more likely to identify with the company as a whole."

In *Made in America,* Dertouzos, Lester, and Solow point out how "organizational hierarchies, with their rigidity and compartmentalization, are an obstacle to cooperation." They go on to say, "They should be replaced with substantially flatter organizational structures that invite communication and cooperation among different corporate departments" (1989, p. 139).

One assumption we can make is that as organizational forms—and the structure of the work conducted within them—continue to move from hierarchies to networks, employees will need to be more cognizant of not only their own activites, but those of others. A new mental set will be needed: one that fosters active and strong identification by employees with their work, co-workers, and the overall organization. A basic proposition that follows is: As an organization's structure moves from hierarchy to network, the need for employee commitment to work, co-worker, and the organization increases concommitantly.

Organizational Controls. The kinds of controls over employee behavior that fit traditional structures tended to be preestablished and formal. There were strictly defined standards and guidelines from which workers were not supposed to deviate; direct supervision served as an ongoing monitor. As long as the demands on the organization for its products and/or services remained relatively unchanging and predictable, the structure and controls remained effective, notwithstanding psychological or social costs to members of the organization.

Most organizations today are dealing with turbulent and unpredictable demands. Consequently, the kinds of controls that are needed, especially in light of the structural transformations that are occurring, must be responsive. The fundamental change in control is related to its locus, which must move from system and supervision to self and social (the individual and group). In short, organizations are moving from compliance, which depends upon system and supervisory control, to commitment, which uses individual and group control. This shift recognizes the need for the organization's informal system to be legitimized as equal to the formal system in serving overall objectives. While a major part of the formal system, including its controls, can continue to be effective for the more routine and predictable aspects of the organization's functions, it is the informal system, with all its flexibility, that can be most responsive to unusual and unexpected demands from the outside world, customers, and the market.

The general proposition offered here is: As an organization's control system moves from system and supervisory control to self and social control, the need for employee commitment to work, co-workers, and organization increases concommitantly.

One can easily see how an organization that restructures itself to be more responsive to change, but fails to modify its methods of control, very likely will defeat its own objectives. For one thing, it will be sending a very mixed and contradictory message to employees: "You are to take initiative and responsibility, but check with your boss before you make a decision or take action.'' Or, ''Be responsive to the customer, but always follow proper procedure.'' Such messages hardly foster the level of commitment that would make a networked organization effective. Furthermore, it is not uncommon for organizational decisions to get stalled by managers who have bought into the new structural arrangement but continue, out of habit, to exercise the same control, thus stifling the initiative of employees who are testing the limits of influence and responsibility. In such circumstances the levels of commitment might remain high within groups and teams, but will not extend to the organization as a whole.

Organizational Climate. The best definition of *organizational climate* I have found is the simplest one, which essentially defines it as ''the feel of the work place.'' This also happens to be the title of the book from which it is borrowed (Steele and Jenks, 1977). The authors identify four key dimensions of climate:

1. The amount of total energy people have available to them.
2. How that energy is distributed or used.
3. The amount of pleasure people get from being in the environment.
4. How much people grow and develop within the system (p. 3).

Climate is perhaps the least tangible aspect of organizational life, but it seems to have very powerful and tangible effects on employees. In a high energy atmosphere one can sense people's excitement just by watching the way they move, the way they interact and go about their business, and even the expressions on their faces. When one walks out of a very positive atmosphere, one wants to go back. If the atmosphere is stifling, unwelcoming, filled with tension, and not much fun, then one does not want to return. If the place happens to be one's workplace, the effect can be very powerful.

Since commitment comes from within the person, the climate in which that person must function is very important. Work or people or organizations that drain energy are likely to result, over the long run, in withdrawal and not in identification. As will be shown in Chapter 4, the two companies that provided the data for the research were very different in organizational climate, which made a critical difference in the research results. The proposition related to climate can be stated as: To the extent that an organization's climate fosters employee pleasure, growth, and development, and to the extent that it energizes its people into actions that serve both individual and organizational purposes, it also tends to foster a high level of employee commitment.

Reward Systems

Purposes Served. An organization's reward system serves five general purposes (Galbraith, 1977):

1. Attracting and holding employees
2. Guaranteeing at least minimal dependable performance
3. Encouraging performance beyond the minimum
4. Encouraging initiative and creativity in employees
5. Promoting collaborative behavior

Insofar as a manager is satisfied to achieve just the first two purposes, compliance will serve that end. To achieve the remaining purposes it is necessary to think in terms of commitment, especially with respect to purposes four and five. It is important to note that a reward system that fosters commitment also will attract and hold employees, as well as obtain at least minimal performance. By way of contrast, a reward system built on compliance is not likely to foster initiative or creativity, much less collaborative behavior. If anything, it fosters competitive and political behavior within the system, usually to the detriment of the organization's effectiveness.

A reward system is made up of the entire array of outcomes that employees are motivated to attain for their performance. Many are tangible and specific, such as wages and benefits; many are specific but not tangible, such as promotions, special recognition, and title changes; still others are more psychological or social (peer approval or appreciation from the boss); and many stem mostly from personal satisfactions and development. What is most important is the connection between the rewards offered and the purposes they serve, as well as the ways in which different rewards either foster or reduce employee commitment in the three categories.

Types of Rewards. There are many theories of motivation relevant to the concept of commitment. However, the most useful and inclusive framework for an organization was offered by Daniel Katz more than twenty-five years ago (1964). With some slight modification in terminology, here is a summary of Katz's framework, followed by a demonstration of how it applies here.

Rewards can be divided into six useful groupings:

1. Compliance with organizational rules and norms
2. General system rewards for all organization members
3. Individual rewards based on merit and performance
4. Social satisfactions from interpersonal relationships
5. Intrinsic satisfactions from task or role performance
6. Internalized values from an organization's purposes.

Now let us examine each grouping and its relationship to the five purposes of a reward system and then to the three dimensions of employee commitment.

1. *Rule Compliance.* Although we usually do not think of following the rules as a form of reward, many people do find rules useful for maintaining a kind of "comfort zone" in their work lives. There is less uncertainty, less fear of being criticized for decisions, and generally a greater sense of clear boundaries and security. Furthermore, it can give one a sense of doing the proper thing and living up to standards of responsibility defined by the system.

Employees who are motivated by rule compliance actually experience themselves as choosing to do so, which seems like a contradiction in terms. The choice they make is to maintain membership in good standing by living within the prescribed rules and norms of the organization. In fact, any deviation from set standards generates personal anxiety, which can only be reduced or avoided in the first place by continued rule compliance.

Major organizations and institutions, such as the military, the church, and many educational settings (a medical school), not only depend upon rule compliance as a part of their reward systems, but actually view it as the very essence of their systems and as fundamental to their survival. It is easy to see how that survival can be threatened when fewer and fewer people choose to live by the rules when they no longer find them rewarding.

Unfortunately, there are those individuals who are so strongly motivated to operate strictly by the rules that they fail to see how their actions subvert the very purposes of the job they were hired to do. I do not need to give examples of people who are so locked in to formal rules that they cannot exercise any reasonable judgment in a situation that may not fit the rule book. Karl Albrecht identifies dependence on the rule book as one of the seven deadly sins of customer service (1988). No doubt the reader can think of many instances of failing to obtain anything close to satisfactory service from an individual who was so self-righteous about the rules as to make the customer feel like a criminal for even suggesting an exception.

An organization that is overdependent on rule compliance is likely, over time, to generate rule *defiance.* I have found this to be especially true of students whose counterdependent tendencies make even the thought of rule compliance unacceptable. Unfortunately for them, a great deal of their education occurs in institutions that do depend upon rule compliance, both in and out of the classroom, as a means of controlling behavior. Compliance is rewarding only for those whose personal goals and values make following the rules fulfilling.

Although rule compliance seems antithetical to commitment, perhaps that is only because of the usual connotation of the term *compliance.* It may seem odd to use a phrase like "commitment to rule compliance" as a way to explain employee behavior, but that is precisely what happens. Many employees who identify strongly with an organization built strongly on traditions tend to internalize all the rules, norms, and customs that maintain those traditions. Furthermore, there tends to be strong identification with work activities that further those organizational ends, as well as with co-workers who share the same belief system.

Rule compliance may effectively attract and hold employees. It also may guarantee at least minimal performance from them, and even some performance beyond the minimum, but rarely will it foster outstanding performance, initiative, creativity, or collaboration, all of which depend upon the freedom to exercise personal judgment in situations that do not fit the rules. Consequently, as a key element of a reward system, rule compliance is valuable for certain kinds of organizations and for potential employees who are attracted to those organizations. In fact, it can serve to foster employee commitment in those cases. However, for most organizations and for most potential employees, it has limited value and even may be obsolete or counterproductive.

2. *General System Rewards.* This class of rewards is familiar to anyone who has worked in an organization of any size. It includes all rewards that accrue to employees as employees. Base salaries or wage scales, health benefits, cost-of-living adjustments, retirement plans, educational benefits, and discounts are examples of general rewards. Since these are important to most people, it is relatively easy to establish an attractive system of very broad-based rewards. They serve to attract and hold employees, and guarantee at least minimal performance. However, because they usually are administered across the board, these rewards tend to have little impact on performance beyond the minimum (except in tight economic times when jobs are scarce), on initiative and creativity, or on collaboration among employees.

In relation to employee commitment, general system rewards tend to have a negative effect when they are inadequate, but have very little positive effect (if any) when they are adequate. For the most part, general rewards are extrinsic and do not strengthen an individual's identification with work, co-workers, or the total system. The rewards are similar to the foundation of a house: It is critical to the rest of the house, but it usually is not tailored to the special needs or characteristics of the owner, at least not to the extent that the rest of the house may be.

3. *Individual Rewards.* This category is probably given the most attention by management today. It is built upon a tradition of economic incentives: People are assumed to be motivated to achieve results that give them the greatest return for their efforts. The return can take many forms, including pay raises, bonuses, promotions, special privileges or opportunities, recognition, and increased power. Although these rewards may be available to all members of the organization, they are administered on an individual basis and, consequently, reinforce individual performance. Unlike general system rewards, individual rewards do foster performance beyond the minimum, initiative, and, to some extent, creativity. However, these rewards do not promote collaborative behavior. They discourage it. In a system that depends

primarily upon individual effort, this may not be a problem, but in one that requires a high degree of worker cooperation and interdependence—as is increasingly the case today—a heavy emphasis on individual rewards can prove to be counterproductive.

Since most rewards in this category are extrinsic and occur only as an outcome of one's work effort, they have little effect on promoting commitment. However, as is the case with general system rewards, when administered improperly, individual rewards can erode any basis for building employee commitment. They often reinforce competitive behavior and feelings among employees, thus reducing the chances of strong co-worker identification and they can easily create the kind of political atmosphere that lowers trust and confidence in upper management.

I am not suggesting that a system of individual incentives is necessarily bad or to be avoided; however, I do want to offer some words of caution. On the one hand, such incentives provide a challenge and stimulate people's drive to achieve and excel; but they also can create obstacles to the kind of collaboration that requires people to act more in the interests of the whole than in their own personal interests. Our society has been built on strong individual drives to achieve, reinforced historically by various forms of individual rewards, usually money, recognition, or promotion. Free enterprise depends upon competition, and the most successful companies are those that attain a competitive edge. Unfortunately, that same sense of competition within an organization can work against its very survival and growth.

Many organizations link their performance appraisal systems to individual rewards. While there is an inherent logic to that, there are also some serious negative consequences. In times of abundant resources managers can feel relatively free to match rewards and performance appropriately; but in times of scarce resources the purposes of appraisals can be subverted easily. It is not uncommon for a company to use a forced distribution in its categories of performance appraisal to control the number and amounts of raises that high performance ratings would demand. In fact, one of the companies that provided the data for my research used just such a system. In contrast, many organizations try to place a developmental emphasis on their performance appraisal systems. Although there may be some financial and promotional rewards for high performance, the individual's learning and career development in the organization are stressed.

4. *Social Satisfactions.* Most jobs today either require or indirectly encourage some level of social interaction among employees. Although many managers still worry that such interactions take time and energy away from getting the job done, most recognize that people are by nature social beings and that satisfying social needs can be one of the great benefits of organizational life. In many instances it is the very glue that keeps employees in what otherwise might be intolerable jobs. Many surveys of workers' needs have

shown that friendly co-workers tend to be one of the most important sources of satisfaction. Especially in difficult times, the presence of supportive colleagues can be what keeps individual employees from leaving.

While not often a factor in attracting employees, social satisfactions are clearly a means of retaining them and even getting at least minimum performance from them. Whether performance beyond the minimum also occurs depends in part on the norms of the group of which a given employee is a member. If the norms support high performance, social bonding will be a major factor in high performance. If not, the organization does not benefit and even may suffer because of a high level of social satisfaction among its employees. The same relationship exists for the other two purposes of a reward system. To the extent that the norms of a work group or the overall system encourage initiative, creativity, and collaboration, strong social rewards add to those ends.

Co-worker identification cannot occur without social satisfaction. In other words, if members of a group, a team, or a department simply do not find it rewarding to work together, it is unlikely (if not impossible) to expect any interpersonal commitment. In some sense this defines the difference between a group and a team, with the latter obviously built upon a foundation of mutual support and caring, as well as on a strong sense of task interdependence.

One point needs to be made about the level of an individual's social need. We all know that some of us require and seek a great deal of social interaction and others very little. These individual differences are important to understanding the role of social satisfaction as a reward and the extent to which it is possible to generate co-worker commitment from an individual. In many cases it is necessary to establish a connection between the outcomes of an effective team effort and the more task- or achievement-related needs of an individual. One of the strongest contributors to a group effort I have run into was almost totally task-oriented and asocial. He clearly recognized and accepted his role, was very strongly committed to his colleagues on a task level, but tended to be painfully uncomfortable in any activities that were purely social.

When it comes to the impact of social satisfaction on commitment to work and commitment to the organization, the connection is indirect. To the extent that one's work is embedded in social interaction, social satisfaction certainly helps to make the work more inviting. However, it is difficult to argue that the individual actually experiences stronger identification with the work itself, apart from the relationships. Similarly, an organization that provides an atmosphere that is socially satisfying may indirectly strengthen employee commitment to it, but this is not the same as creating conditions that foster an employee's sense of personal identification with the purposes and identity of the organization.

5. *Intrinsic Satisfactions.* When it comes to human motivation, work that provides intrinsic satisfaction is probably the most self-sustaining. The reward for doing it is built into the activity and requires little else, short of a supportive work setting, to keep one going. Almost by definition it fosters a high level of commitment, since it embodies a connection between the work and the worker. When employees are matched to jobs that give them intrinsic satisfaction, managers usually find that their performance is high and little supervision is required.

While some jobs offer little chance for intrinsic satisfaction, there are many that, if redesigned properly, could be shaped to the style and needs of the worker. Unfortunately, too many managers fail to see opportunities for job redesign and also do not recognize that employees often are the first to see those opportunities. The next chapter discusses some approaches to work redesign, all of which stress the importance of intrinsic satisfaction.

In achieving the goals of a reward system, intrinsic satisfaction goes a long way toward attracting and holding employees (assuming that they anticipate that the work will be intrinsically rewarding), does foster performance beyond the minimum, and does encourage initiative and creativity, at least in relation to the work itself. It does not, however, promote collaborative behavior; in fact, a highly absorbing task can work against collaboration unless employees make a conscious effort to stress their roles in the larger effort.

Although job satisfaction and commitment are not the same, intrinsic satisfaction from the job is, as noted, the essence of identification with work. Only to the extent that the work requires cooperation among co-workers does intrinsic satisfaction also promote co-worker identification. And only to the extent that the individual's and organization's needs and values are congruent does intrinsic satisfaction promote organizational identification. However, it takes a deliberate effort by management to establish and maintain both connections: to make certain that the work is perceived by the worker as part of a cooperative effort of the group and of the organization.

6. *Internalized Organizational Values.* Volunteer organizations are perhaps the best example of people whose rewards come primarily from believing in what the organization stands for, its mission or purposes. Some companies and institutions naturally fall into this category and others do not. For example, I have spoken to many employees who work in service organizations, including medical settings, insurance companies, and banks, and feel that they are part of something that is making a difference to people, serving some useful purpose in society, making life better for their customers or clients. I also have had conversations with workers on the shop floor of a manufacturing company who believe that the company is producing a quality product, something they can be proud of, and that they are contributing to that end. By way of contrast, I have spoken to employees who perform well but who are totally indifferent to, and certainly not proud of, the product

or service their employer provides to the world. People who choose professional careers usually do so because of some connection between their personal aspirations and values and those of their professions. Those individuals usually are employed by organizations that represent those same goals and values.

Probably the most important aspect of the category of internalized values as a source of reward is that it tends to serve all five purposes of a reward system. This is not to suggest that it is the only set of rewards needed to achieve those purposes, but that internalized values can make a substantial difference. What is also significant is that this category promotes and enhances collaboration insofar as the majority of employees shares the same goals and values. It seems to provide the overarching objective that enables employees to see beyond their individual jobs and even beyond departmental boundaries.

While intrinsic rewards generate identification with work and social rewards help broaden that identification to the team level, internalized values are the principal source of identification with the organization. To the extent that a high commitment system is important to management, organizational leadership must pay attention to the full range of rewards, but especially to whatever it takes to link employees' goals and values to those of the organization as a whole. Employees in a high performance organization not only perceive their value to the system, but also need to perceive the value of the organization in its environment.

Thus far the following points have been made about the relationship between rewards and the purposes they serve. At best, rule compliance may attract and hold employees and obtain at least minimum performance. However, this source of reward is unlikely to result in performance beyond the minimum, in initiative and creativity, or in collaboration.

General rewards tend to attract and hold employees, obtain at least minimum performance, but rarely serve as an incentive for performance beyond the minimum, initiative, creativity, or collaborative effort.

Individual rewards attract and hold employees, obtain at least minimal performance, and foster performance beyond the minimum, initiative, and creativity. They do not, however, tend to result in collaboration.

Social rewards may or may not attract employees, but they do serve to hold them in the organization and obtain at least minimum performance from them. Whether they result in performance beyond the minimum, in initiative and creativity, or in collaboration depends considerably on group and organizational standards related to performance.

Intrinsic rewards tend to serve all purposes except collaboration. However, they also can strengthen collaboration to the extent that the work requires task interdependence and has real value relative to the organization's goals and values.

Internalized values tend to serve all purposes, including collaborative effort, because the employee's highest priority is attaining personal goals that are congruent with organizational goals.

It is important for managers to recognize that they need to be clear about what purposes they want a reward system to serve and then consider the range of options available. In most complex systems today, all six categories may be relevant, since the range of individual needs and values is wide and varied. Similarly, it is important for a manager to consider the kind and level of employee commitment that best fits the organization. Later chapters consider various commitment profiles that may help with this task, but consider for now the following propositions:

- To the extent that commitment to the work is desired, it is necessary (but not sufficient) to provide general and individual rewards, but intrinsic rewards are both necessary and sufficient.

- To the extent that commitment to co-workers is desired, it is necessary (but not sufficient) to provide social rewards and general rewards; it may be important to de-emphasize individual rewards; it may be necessary to emphasize task interdependence as part of intrinsic satisfaction; whether it is necessary to generate internalization of organizational values depends upon the degree of sub-unit interdependence that exists.

- To the extent that commitment to the organization is desired, it is necessary (but not sufficient) to provide general, individual, social, and intrinsic rewards, but it is most necessary, and usually sufficient, to foster internalization of organizational values. Rule compliance can be a contributing factor, but it also can result in behavior that is mistaken for true commitment.

Employee Performance

Measuring employee performance has been a managerial dilemma since the beginning of organizational life. In times gone by, one could simply count the number of stones laid, trees cut, or pies baked in order to know how productive a worker was. Even during the early part of this century it was possible for a supervisor to use simple quantitative measures of performance: parts assembled, holes drilled, or people served. The task of measuring performance has become much more complicated for a variety of reasons. Work has become more complex and has required more frequent employee interaction and cooperation; situations change frequently and often unpredictably; and there has been an increasing emphasis on quality, not just quantity. The net result has been that performance appraisals now are based upon a constellation of factors that somehow add up to single judgment, and usually a subjective one at that. Despite every attempt to make appraisals objective and fair, they remain essentially subjective and biased.

Add to this the trend toward participative management and self-managing teams. Who makes the judgments about an employee's contribution to the team effort or an individual's contribution to the quality of a decision? How does one measure the quality of customer service and separate the behavior of a valued employee and the chronic complaining of a customer?

A human resources manager at a large insurance company said in reference to the company's evaluation system: "I've given up. No matter how we redesign the system, somebody says it's no good. It's either too rigid and number-oriented, or it isn't clearly enough defined, or it's unfair to people whose jobs are changing, or the supervisor has too much input, or the employee has too much input. You can't win. We worked for over a year developing this approach, we finally have all the forms and procedures nailed down, and we're told to go back and make major changes. I just don't see how we can improve on it, but I have no choice. Any ideas, Mr. Consultant?"

As it happened, I did not at that time have a remedy for that situation, but it pointed out to me that any attempt to design a performance appraisal system in organizations today faces a variety of almost impossible dilemmas. First of all, evaluations are an inherently subjective process in which people make judgments about other people. How fair those judgments are is always a matter of whom one asks. The person doing the evaluation believes it is fair and objective; the person being judged usually agrees if the evaluation is positive and disagrees if it is negative. Many companies resort to presumably objective quantitative indices such as minutes late to work or days absent. But even those are questionable in light of the changes in work patterns and the degree to which workers on the shop floor are being given more responsibility for managing themselves.

In addition, an inherent conflict is emerging between the traditional emphasis of evaluations on individual performance and the newer and increasing emphasis on teamwork. How do we merge the two philosophies? Would it be enough for the individual to know that he or she has made a valuable contribution to the team and to the organization and yet see only the team receive recognition? But if the emphasis remains on recognizing the individual performer, what does that do to collaboration among team members? In Japan there is a saying that the nail that sticks up gets hammered down. How would that idea sit with American workers? Not too well, I would imagine. The solution probably resides in some combination or integration of performance measures that place equal value on the individual's contribution to the team's work and the quality of the team's performance.

Here is where we can learn something from sports. An assist in basketball or hockey is recognized because it contributes to the score, even though the person who made the assist is not the one who is credited directly with the points that help win the game. This system encourages team effort, not grandstanding. A similar approach might be applied to performance appraisal and, in fact, is being adopted in some organizations. It is certainly more complicated than the assist in sports because there are many intangibles that need to be considered.

For example, how is a team member credited with helping to foster a positive spirit in the group? What recognition is to be given to those who facilitate the group's work and participation of its members? Some organizations have made peer review part of performance evaluation and include in the evaluation criteria a wide range of behavior that may be related either to the task or teamwork. Insofar as the group has a high level of trust and openness among members, this can work; in their absence, peer review can be relatively ineffective and may damage group members. An example of a team-centered, performance-appraisal system using peer evaluations is discussed in Chapter 10.

A critical issue is the impact of performance appraisals on employee commitment. To the extent that the evaluation increases the individual's attention to external pressures and extrinsic rewards, it can easily detract from any effort to build employee identification with work, co-workers, or the organization: they require attention to the intrinsic satisfactions of work and its contribution to the overall effort. Instead of resulting in commitment, which has its own sustaining force, the typical appraisal results in compliance, which generates employee dependence on outside direction and guidance.

A commitment-centered approach to performance evaluation is necessary in an organization that is moving toward employee participation and greater teamwork. Chapter 6 offers some guidelines for developing such an approach and several examples of companies that seem to be making progress.

The two companies used in the main body of the research for this book had traditional performance appraisal systems that used a range of categories into which every employee was placed. The evaluations represented the final judgments of supervisors based upon a variety of criteria. Although the methods were not consistent with the principles of a commitment-based system, they were the only measures of employee performance available for the study. I assumed that whatever faults, biases, or inconsistencies might exist in either company's system, the ratings would be valid enough to distinguish the best from the worst employees overall.

With respect to the relationship between performance appraisal and commitment, the following propositions apply:

- To the extent that a performance appraisal process is related to the unique abilities of the individual, emphasizes learning and development, and encourages self-management, it tends to foster a high level of employee commitment to the work.

- To the extent that a performance appraisal process is related to an individual's contribution to the team effort, it tends to foster a high level of commitment to co-workers.

- To the extent that a performance appraisal process is related to the individual's contribution to meeting organizational goals that are also personal goals, it tends to foster a high level of commitment to the organization.

The conclusion is this: *Employee commitment increases the level of employee performance.*

The clearest and perhaps the most critical connection is between performance and commitment, with the appraisal process providing the link. However, a high level of employee performance—difficult as it may be to measure in today's complex work settings—still represents the principal outcome sought by managers. The conceptual framework used here only highlights the ways in which the various elements of an organization (its management practices, its reward system, and the commitment of its employees) contribute to that outcome.

Chapter 3

Historical Roots

Most new ideas have historical roots and are new only in the sense that they redefine a way of looking at things. When I developed the three-dimensional model of commitment, it was evident to me that it represented a fusion of concepts that I had been using for many years and that these concepts came from three different lines of thought. One line of thought related to theories of individual behavior, especially motivation; a second line related to group behavior and dynamics; the third pertained to concepts of organizational leadership. It is useful to trace the three lines of thought in order to place my model in the context of emerging ideas. This chapter provides a summary of the history and a brief review of previous research on commitment.

The Turn of the Century

With the Industrial Revolution came mass production and the assembly line. The major concern of the corporation was productivity, with primary emphasis on quantity and efficiency. Frederick Taylor (1915) was a major figure influencing management practices in the early part of the twentieth century. What Taylor introduced, in his "scientific management" approach to work design, was a way to maximize productivity and efficiency. Taylor's emphasis was on clear task differentiation, with workers being trained to perform very specific tasks, usually simple and repetitive, as precisely as possible. The worker was essentially part of the machinery of production. The nature of the work itself required little, if any, judgment from the worker.

In the early 1900s, most workers were poorly educated. Consequently, management did all the thinking and the worker all the doing. Furthermore, production was built in serial order with each step highly controllable and predictable. Since the work flow was designed to allow little variation, the worker was required to perform as closely as possible to machine standards. For those times and conditions, the mechanistic model proved highly effective and efficient.

Taylor's approach also had humanistic elements. The precise division of labor permitted management to establish the best fit between worker and job, thereby enabling the organization to pay workers decent wages for satisfactory performance. Although many industries were exploitive, that certainly was not Taylor's intent. His objectives included maximum production and the fair treatment of workers (Weisbord, 1987).

Mid-Century

In the 1930s and 1940s the Hawthorne studies demonstrated that worker performance is affected as much by peer pressure as by management requirements (Roethlisberger and Dickson, 1939). Workers were better educated and more conscious of human needs other than money. The informal social processes of the workplace became recognized as a strong influence on the behavior of the worker.

The Hawthorne studies demonstrated just how powerful group norms can be in determining productivity. They also heralded a major change in thinking about organizations as social systems. In the context of this book, the turn of the century focused almost exclusively on the work itself, but failed to look at the issue of worker commitment; evidently, compliance with job requirements was enough. When the informal forces of the social system were "discovered," the significance of co-worker commitment became evident. The next phase proved most interesting: It represented a recognition of the relationship between the work being done and the social system doing it.

The late 1940s saw some fundamental changes in the way work was carried out in, of all places, the coal mines in England. Guided by the research of the Tavistock Institute, coalminers were organized into work teams, instead of the "single worker at a single task" (Trist and Bamforth, 1951).

The notion behind the change was that the technical aspects of the work could be carried out using various worker arrangements (i.e., the social aspects of the work) and that the job of management was to develop the best possible match between the two so that the needs of the technical and the social systems were met. This was the beginning of the *sociotechnical approach* to work design. It is important to note that growth of the sociotechnical approach was paralleled by a growth in interest and research in *group dynamics* that began in the 1940s and has continued into the 1990s. Many of the same people have contributed to both areas.

Several other changes resulted in major transformations of thinking about organizations and work arrangements. The levels of knowledge and sophistication required to conduct work in the 1960s and 1970s increased almost too rapidly to comprehend. No longer did managers alone possess the information, knowledge, or expertise to make the highly complex decisions necessary to complete jobs. No longer did managers have levels of educational significantly higher than a large percentage of the work force. By 1980, the so-called lower levels of companies were full of people with training and ability greater than those of upper management.

Failure to acknowledge the situation and adapt to it resulted in deterioration of work standards and a general decline in the quantity and quality of work performed. In such cases, management failed to create conditions that would maximize employee commitment. Instead, management continued to rely on compliance. To this day there are major corporations that cling to compliance, that fail to appreciate the changes and opportunities that have occurred. In not seeing beyond the technical objectives of the work, they miss taking advantage of alternatives in work design.

The 1960s and Beyond

Work Redesign

The turning point in managerial thinking in this country occurred in the late 1950s and early 1960s with the appearance of the writings of Herzberg (1959), McGregor (1960), and Likert (1961). Herzberg changed ways of viewing workers' motivation, McGregor changed managerial assumptions about workers' attitudes toward work, and Likert provided a whole new way of looking at a manager's role. The combination was a powerful complement to the sociotechnical thinking already making its mark. A new paradigm had emerged; it required a new way of looking at work design and new models of organizational leadership.

Perhaps the most significant shift from the job simplification model to a more enlightened view of how work can best be carried out came with the research of Fred Herzberg in the 1950s and 1960s. Herzberg emphasized the enlargement and enrichment of work as the most effective means to increase worker productivity. While the results generally were positive for productivity, attractiveness of the work, worker retention, morale, and worker development, there were some unanticipated costs. The approach required more training, gave employees a greater sense of their own power (not always appreciated by management) and it raised expectations that more changes would follow, which was not always the case.

By the early 1970s the new view was evident in the work of Hackman and Lawler (1971) and later in that of Hackman and Oldham (1980), who added a major step in the direction of job redesign. Their research identified five key elements of a job that result in high motivation: *autonomy, feedback, skill variety, task identity (doing the whole job),* and *task significance (job has impact on others).* Efforts to redesign work to maximize these elements had very positive effects on performance and satisfaction, but with costs similar to those for job enrichment.

What enlightened management had to recognize, and in many cases did, was that the immediate costs of these changes would be more than offset by the long-term gains. The significant variables are employees' identification with the work and, depending on how the work is redesigned, employees' identification with co-workers and/or organization. For example, using self-managing work teams is a way of strengthening commitment both to work and co-workers.

Work Groups and Teams

The proliferation of research on small groups after World War II was staggering. The Hawthorne findings became the impetus for a major movement in social psychology and group dynamics. Business and industry rapidly applied what the academics were learning. George Homans (1950) and Kurt Lewin (1951) provided solid and systematic work; meanwhile organizational consultants were excited about the potential power of group dynamics to change organizations. In their enthusiasm many practitioners applied their newly discovered methods indiscriminately and often inappropriately. This is not to suggest that the group methods of the 1960s and 1970s were flawed. Quite the contrary. Much of it was based upon very sound theory and well-conceived application. The problems occurred when the demand for application to organizational problems accelerated faster than the knowledge about how to apply group methods effectively.

There was no question about the potential of group forces to shape individual performance. The questions were how to understand those forces and make effective use of them without manipulating people outright. Homans' work helped us understand the relationships among the basic dynamics that operate in a group, including what is required of members, what they bring to the situation, the context in which they are working, and what inevitably emerges in relation to a group's productivity, satisfaction, and development. The incredible power of group norms, revealed in the Hawthorne studies, is given major emphasis in Homans' work.

Not long after the pioneering research in the British coal mines, the Scandinavian car manufacturers Saab and Volvo successfully introduced the team as an alternative to the traditional assembly line. Teams were given responsibility for assembling automobiles, with the freedom to govern their own work with minimal supervision. In the 1960s and 1970s, the team model was picked up in the United States by a number of major corporations, including TRW, General Electric, Digital Equipment Corporation, Proctor and Gamble, and many others. Perhaps its most notable use of teams in the 1980s was in Ford's Taurus plants.

The new approach contained many elements in the kind of effective work design described by Hackman and others and consequently resulted in the same desired outcomes. However, because the team approach addressed issues related to both the work itself and the relationships among the workers, it directly affected two dimensions of commitment—work and people. It probably indirectly affected organizational commitment because the teams could see the finished product before it went out the door. In recent years at Volvo, the teams have been permitted to have direct contact with customers for orders, delivery, and follow-up. This kind of responsibility clearly helps to foster employees' identification with the mission of the company. In short, the beauty of the sociotechnical model is that it clearly affects both work and co-worker commitment and may affect organizational commitment.

Many efforts to build teams at any level focus exclusively on relationships. When used appropriately, the results can be very positive. Members of a team learn to listen to each other, respect their differences, use their human resources, manage their time, improve the group's performance, and learn from mistakes. The norms foster cooperation, mutual support, and attention to both task and social needs of the team. When organizations talk about team building, those are the kinds of goals they usually have in mind.

Other team-building efforts may take broader aim, including attention to organizational structure, the influences of the company climate, and the physical setting. This view recognizes that groups, like individuals, do not exist in isolation, but as part of a larger, more complex system. Team building, from this perspective, emphasizes the importance of the larger context, how the team can manage itself in relation to that context, and when necessary, influence it. One manufacturing plant was frustrated that its months of team building on the shop floor were not having the results anticipated. When management discussed the problem with the workers, they stated that they really needed more direct control over the layout of the jobs and the arrangement of the equipment. The supervisor said, "This teamwork stuff isn't worth a damn if we can't even see each other on the job." The workers' request was honored, and the results were dramatic, much to the satisfaction of management.

This example demonstrates the importance of defining team building in terms of the relationships of team members and the team's autonomy in defining its own work arrangements. These workers were empowered to determine the design of the work itself and the process by which the group managed itself. This was a truly effective implementation of sociotechnical thinking and certainly one that should strengthen worker identification with both the task and the team.

Northern Telecom, in Morrisville, N.C., is an excellent example of a company that has extended its teamwork effort beyond the boundaries of the teams themselves. Its team approach to managing was motivated by employees and built around a common vision. One employee was quoted as saying, "We can be better than we are." A key element that helps Northern Telecom maintain a total organizational focus and offset the narrower perspective that each team might develop is what the company calls the "round table," which is a group of employees, representing all aspects of the company, that meets regularly to focus on organization-wide problems.

System Development and Leadership

While team-building efforts have done much to increase the quantity and quality of performance in the various departments of an organization, it has become increasingly important for top management, especially in large organizations, to pay attention to system integration and create an environment in which there is continuous collaboration across departmental and divisional boundaries. The kind of leadership that can envision and articulate overarching goals and future possibilities is required more and more. Organizational leaders who have come up through the ranks and remain committed primarily to their professional roots (e.g., engineering, sales, finance) often fail to provide that broad vision, unless they have learned to step out of their narrow perspectives and into larger world views.

The 1970s witnessed an increasing volume of literature on the subject of organizational leadership. There seemed to be a quest for a model of the ideal leader. While situational leadership was viewed as the most practical way of thinking about the issue, somehow we were not satisfied that we fully understood the concept of leadership. Although it was common to assert that there is no one best way to lead, many scholars who continued to search for a concept of leadership came closer to defining it in terms that fit most, if not all, situations. In fact, Blake and Mouton disavowed the situational model and advocated a leadership style that emphasized strong attention to both task and people as the one best approach (1982). By the mid-1980s, several other major writers and researchers were developing leadership models that seemed to capture the issues in new and exciting ways.

The idea of *developmental leadership* (Bradford and Cohen, 1984) added a new dimension to managerial thinking, helping managers to see beyond what the authors called *heroic models* of leadership. The concept of *visionary leadership* seemed to capture the imagination not only of practicing managers and executives, but also of the public at large. The descriptions of highly successful corporate and institutional leaders provided by Bennis and Nanus (1985) gave us a vivid picture of just how the vision of a leader gets translated into the success of an enterprise. The writings of Bass (1985) and later the work of Kouzes and Pozner (1987) gave us the concept of *transformational leadership,* in contrast to the more traditional *transactional leadership.* The former uses empowerment of people as the principal basis of influence; the latter depends more on the use of rewards and punishments. In the context of this book, it is the developmental, visionary, transformational leader who generates employee commitment, while the more heroic, controlling, transactional leader fosters compliance.

In his research on executives, Gareth Morgan noted that despite a wide variety of personality types, "they all converged on the importance of understanding the leadership process in terms of *shared values, shared direction,* and *shared responsibility* for the future of the organization" (1988, p. 52). It is this form of leadership that, according to Morgan, will generate the energy and commitment that will be needed to drive organizations in the future. However, it takes much more than a philosophy to generate organizational commitment; it takes carefully orchestrated actions that reinforce the connections among the various parts of the system.

Top leaders have a strong advantage, says John Gardner in *On Leadership* (1990). Gardner states, "Leaders have the capacity to mobilize lower-level leaders within the system and to reach out to potential allies at all levels. With respect to most of the initiatives the leader wishes to take, there will be numbers of individuals down through the organization who are wholehearted allies, and the leader can often activate them regardless of intervening resistance in the chain of command. Leaders can turn on green lights throughout the organization with a minimum expenditure of energy" (p. 91).

What both Morgan and Gardner are describing is leadership behavior that fosters a high level of organizational commitment, an identification not just with one's own job and territory, and not exclusively with one's department and professional group, but with the purposes and future directions of the whole system.

Bennis and Nanus (1985) talk about the "commitment gap," which is the failure of leaders to instill vision, meaning, and trust in their followers—a failure to empower them. That gap, according to the authors, cannot be filled through dialogue and verbal compliance alone; it requires that the vision be articulated clearly and frequently in a variety of ways. It is filled only when the vision and all that goes with it become a way of thinking.

Robert Heller (1984) emphasizes the leader's visibility to employees as a major factor in empowerment, along with the value of staying in close touch with employees' needs and realities. And Peter Drucker, in *The Effective Executive* (1966), stresses the importance of the leader's being aware of her or his own contribution to the whole organization and its purpose, as well as being aware of the development of others.

In general, then, we can appreciate the overwhelming significance of strong and effective leadership in building strong employee identification with an organization. In some respects the individual may identify as much or more with the person in the leadership position than with the organization itself, especially if that leader is charismatic. Usually, identification spills over to what that leader represents and, consequently, does instill strong company commitment. When there is no carry-over to company commitment, individuals are likely to find their work strongly affected by the leader's behavior, and performance may even deteriorate when the leader is no longer occupying the top position.

Heads of family businesses, entrepreneurs, and many creators of direct sales organizations find that their presence, or at least accessibility, tends to have a visible effect on employees' behavior (Biggart, 1989). Truly effective leaders or managers pay attention to all aspects of employee behavior and create an environment that fosters commitment on all three fronts.

Thus, the three dimensions of commitment each are rooted in different historical lines. Commitment to work has its roots in the theories and research that focus on the way in which individual work is carried out, beginning with Taylor's scientific management and continuing through current concepts of job redesign. Commitment to co-workers has its roots in research on small groups, beginning with the Hawthorne experiments and manifested today in the emphasis on team building at all levels of an organization. The roots of commitment to the total organization are not, surprisingly, as deep as one might think. Although the concept of *loyalty* probably is older than the pharoahs, the idea of true organizational commitment has been an outgrowth of the new styles of leadership. A competent transactional leader certainly can buy loyalty, perhaps even for a worker's lifetime, if the rewards are great enough. However, identification with an organization's purpose or mission is not something a leader or manager can buy. It is the result of an internalized connection between oneself and the organization. Leaders who empower through involvement and through a shared vision engender commitment, not loyalty, at least in the traditional sense.

Recent Research on Commitment

Rather than present a complete review of the literature, I decided to cover only those studies that are most directly related to my own work. There are a number of studies referred to in subsequent chapters, especially Chapter 6, which discuss the results of my research. Many are not discussed in this chapter.

Except for an article by Becker in 1960, no significant research specific to the concept of commitment appeared until almost 1970. Kanter's work on the topic between 1968 and 1972, that of Brown in 1969, Hall, Schneider, and Nygren in 1970, Sheldon in 1971, and Hrebiniak and Alutto in 1972 represented the beginning of a significant period of research on the topic. This continued throughout the 1970s and into the middle of the 1980s, after which very little appeared on the topic, except for several review articles.

Instead of covering this material chronologically, it is discussed in relation to those factors most pertinent to the topic of commitment. Included are employee age, tenure, gender, position in the organization, management style, education, employee rewards and expectations, and performance. This approach provides a more natural introduction to the chapters that follow and also are of greater practical value to readers, especially those who are practicing managers.

Age and Tenure

Both age and tenure (i.e., years with the organization) have been found to relate positively to commitment to the organization, as well as to each other. In other words, employees who have remained with a company for many years tend to be more committed and also are older than those who have been hired more recently. This set of relationships is more likely to occur in companies that promote from within, so it is difficult to generalize outside that context. However, it is possible that each factor, age and tenure, relates independently to commitment. In the research conducted for this book, described in Chapter 5 and discussed in Chapter 6, this question will be examined further.

Gender

There is evidence that women are more committed to an organization than men are (Angle and Perry, 1981; Hrebiniak and Alutto, 1972). Given that there still are serious barriers to women in today's organizations (barriers that keep a disproportionate percentage of women in the lower ranks), it is surprising to find the level of organizational commitment to be higher in women than in men. In fact, this finding runs counter to all expectations, since we usually associate high commitment levels with greater opportunity, responsibility, and self-management. The results of my own research shed some light on the specific aspects of commitment that differentiate men and women.

Position (Level) in the Organization and Management Style

While some research suggests that one's level in the organization has little bearing on commitment to that organization, there is considerable evidence that decision-making power and degree of job autonomy definitely are related to commitment (Morris and Steers, 1980). In most settings one's level in the organization is related directly to level of responsibility and authority in making decisions, so it would follow that position also would correlate with commitment.

An exception to this scenario might arise where decision-making has been decentralized—where employee participation is high. In such a case there might be little difference in commitment levels as a function of organizational level, not so much because upper levels are less committed, but because lower levels are more committed. Several studies have shown that worker autonomy and self-control tend to result in higher levels of employee commitment (Buchanan, 1974; Hall, Schneider, and Nygren, 1970; Marsh and Mannari, 1977). In more structural terms, it also has been found that decentralization of control relates positively to employee commitment (Steers and Porter, 1974; Stevens, Beyer, and Trice, 1978).

Educational Level

The data on education have very important implications. In several studies educational level was found to relate *negatively* to commitment (Morris and Steers, 1980; Angle and Perry, 1981). In other words, an organization can expect less commitment from its most educated members, even though these are the very people it might be most dependent upon for its success. This picture is consistent with what we see in modern organizations, especially high tech companies and other settings (e.g., medical and educational) in which advanced degrees in highly specialized areas of expertise are valued. Commitment in such contexts is more related to one's profession than to the particular setting in which that profession is practiced. The more advanced one's degree, the greater is one's mobility and attractiveness to other organizations. The extent of job hopping among professionals with advanced degrees is testimony to this principle.

Since the commitment model offered here differentiates identification with one's work from identification with one's organization, we will be able to see how the individual's level of education relates to the different dimensions of commitment.

Employees' Expectations about Rewards

Explanations of employee behavior that stress the importance of meeting expectations are built around a transactional model of management. Some authors, including me, have attempted to differentiate expectancy from commitment as a source of motivation, because commitment stems from an internalized process (Scott and Hart, 1981; Wiener, 1982). However, several studies have shown a positive relationship between the degree to which employees' expectations are met and the level of employees' commitment (Steers, 1977; Stevens, 1978; Morris and Sherman, 1981). That the two factors are related may not imply any cause-effect relationship, but may be a consequence of management practices that place high priority both on meeting employees' expectations and creating conditions that foster identification with the organization.

Employee Performance

Previous studies found the relationship between commitment and performance to be weak at best (Mowday, Porter, and Dubin, 1974; Steers, 1977; Crampton et al., 1978). A number of explanations has been offered, most emphasizing that many other variables influence performance and that commitment itself, while significant, may not be a major factor. What I hope to do is shed some light on this question through the use of measures that differentiate the type of commitment. It is quite possible, perhaps even likely, that the relationship between performance and commitment is specific to one dimension and is not clearly reflected in general measures.

In summary, we can say that organizational commitment has been found to relate positively to age and tenure, is higher in women than in men, is unrelated to one's level in the organization, relates positively to degree of autonomy and responsibility, relates negatively to educational level, is higher for employees whose expectations are met, and is positively, though not strongly, related to performance. These variables, along with several others, were studied for this book. The important difference from previous research, however, was the opportunity to study them in relation to each specific dimension of commitment.

Chapter 4

How to Measure and Study Commitment

This chapter describes the steps involved in developing the measures of commitment, and the methods used to conduct the research, including descriptions of the companies that were studied and the additional data gathered on the companies.

Creating the Commitment Diagnosis Instrument (CDI)

To create an instrument that would measure commitment in terms close to the realities of the workplace and meaningful to practicing managers, I decided to generate the items directly from the experiences of managers themselves. Using a series of management education programs held over two years at the University of New Hampshire, it was possible to generate the items that became the finished instrument. The procedure was simple and direct.

I started with the assumption that commitment can only be *inferred* from the behavior and attitudes of employees themselves. This assumption translated into the following question: "What would one expect to see employees doing (or not doing) and saying (or not saying) that would reflect an identification with their work, co-workers, or the organization as a whole?"

Following a presentation of the concept of commitment, including an explanation of identification and distinctions among the three dimensions of commitment, a group of managers (usually 15 to 18) was divided into three smaller groups. Each group was instructed to generate a list of the kinds of behavior and attitudes it would expect to see or hear from employees who identified strongly with their work, their co-workers, or their organization, depending on the category assigned to the group. Each group presented its list to the total group for clarification and discussion, ending up with a list in each category that best represented a consensus. In a number of instances, an item was stated in negative terms: what one would *not* expect to see or hear from a highly committed employee. (For example, watching the clock was considered a sign of low identification with work.)

The final list that formed the basis of the Commitment Diagnosis Instrument (CDI) included only items that appeared in at least three out of four sessions. A given item might have been worded slightly different in the various sessions, but it was easy enough to determine equivalent meanings. For example, a phrase like "taking pride in the quality of one's work" could be considered equivalent to "making sure that one's work is the best." The CDI ended up with thirty items, ten in each category.

The final list of items for the CDI was created from the phrases shown here.

Identification with Work

- Becoming absorbed in one's work to the point of shutting out everything else.
- Great enjoyment of one's work.
- Taking pride in the quality of one's work.
- Not watching the clock in order to leave on time.
- The workday not dragging and seeming endless.
- Being able to concentrate and shut out other things.
- Thinking about work even when not at work.
- Work being a major source of need satisfaction.
- Finding that the work itself is its own reward.
- Constant efforts to improve one's skills in the job.

Identification with Co-Workers

- Being aware of how others are doing in their work.
- Being ready to help co-workers when necessary.
- Not taking a "mind your own business" attitude.
- Looking forward to seeing one's co-workers.
- Willingness to mix work and friendship.
- Letting a co-workers' needs come before one's own.
- Making an effort to stay connected with co-workers on the job.
- Finding real satisfaction from interacting with co-workers.
- Seeing co-workers as "family" on the job.
- Making efforts to welcome new co-workers to the job.

Identification with the Organization

- Taking pleasure in the successes of the organization.
- Seeking information on how the organization is doing overall.
- Seeing the organization's goals as congruent with one's own goals.
- Knowing how one's own work contributes to the total effort.
- Paying attention to the work flow beyond departmental lines.
- Feeling defensive when someone criticizes one's organization.
- Letting organizational priorities take precedent over departmental.
- Not seeing other organizations as "greener pastures."
- Tending to cast one's own organization in an ideal light.
- Feeling strongly about the behavior of the organization's CEO.

The phrases were converted to complete statements and organized into a thirty-item, seven-point rating scale. Each statement on the scale is judged by the subject according to the degree to which it is true for that person. Half the items in the instrument are stated positively, so that a higher score reflects greater commitment; half the items are stated negatively, so that a higher score reflects less commitment. The mixture of positive and negative statements was used to prevent any patterns that might lead a subject to automatically circle numbers down one side or the other of the scale. Also, the positive and negative statements were mixed randomly, not systematically, again to avoid any pattern. (The CDI is available directly from the author and may be used only with written permission.)

Chapter 7 explores ways to use the measures of commitment as a tool for organizational change and development. This is covered in two ways: One part of the chapter is devoted to the formal use of the instrument (the CDI) to provide data for diagnosing a large system, as well as for gathering data and diagnosing a small system (group); another part of the chapter discusses more informal methods, emphasizing observation and interaction. For the informal approach we will look at how the phrases in Figures 4.1 to 4.3 can serve as *commitment indicators* in the same way that the CDI uses scaled items to generate quantifiable measures for research purposes. Whether the formal or informal approach is taken may be left to the consultant or investigator, depending upon the purposes for which the data are to be used. As will be shown, using any measures of employee commitment to improve an organization can best be done as *action-research* in which the data are used as feedback and, consequently, to guide interventions.

Pilot Study

A pilot study was conducted to test the internal consistency of the instrument. A sample of one hundred individuals selected from the executive programs mentioned earlier, middle managers in a bank, and professional staff at the university filled out the CDI. A split-half (odd-numbered versus even-numbered items) reliability of 0.81 was obtained for the total instrument (see Appendix B for an explanation of reliability). In a subsample of one hundred individuals randomly selected at a later date from the main body of the research the split-half correlation was 0.80. No attempt was made to establish internal consistency for the separate categories because the number of odd or even items (five) was too small to produce stable figures.

As an additional check on internal consistency, correlations were computed among the three categories and for each category with the total score. Table 4.1 shows the results.

It should be noted that while all correlations were significant and in most cases quite strong, the relationships between commitment to work and commitment to the organization were greater than the relationship between co-worker commitment and either of the other two categories. Also, the work and organization dimensions both turned out to be better predictors of total scores than did co-worker commitment. Another way to interpret these comparisons is that commitment to one's co-workers tends to be a more independent category of commitment than the other two. As the results reported in Chapter 5 show, this is an important aspect of the relationship among the three categories.

Development of the Research

Background

The main body of data was obtained in collaboration with Dr. Susan Herman, a faculty member in organizational behavior at the Keene State campus of the University of New Hampshire system. Dr. Herman was researching the concept of company spirit, which she defines very broadly as reflecting pride in one's company, a positive organizational climate, a common sense of purpose, pleasure and positive challenge in the work of the organization, security in the work environment, and the feeling of reciprocal support among the members of management (1991). Dr. Herman's approach was not quantitative; it was designed around in-depth interviews related to her theoretical constructs. Consequently, it appeared to both of us that our projects could be combined usefully with respect to the data to be gathered and that the combination of quantitative and qualitative approaches could complement each other well. Although this book will not present the results

Table 4.1

Correlations among the Three Commitment Categories for
both Companies Studied

Dimensions	Company A	Company B
Work & co-worker	.44	.47
Work & organization	.56	.66
Work & total score	.83	.86
Co-worker & organization	.48	.52
Co-worker & total score	.75	.77
Organization & total score	.84	.88

of Dr. Herman's research, it will refer in very general terms to the similarities and differences we found in comparing the two companies.

The Two Companies

The two organizations (identified as Company A and Company B) used for data collection were similar in many respects. They were both manufacturing firms with about six hundred employees in their United States plants; both used advanced technology in their production processes; both were multinational; both had fairly strong promotion-from-within policies; and both served as principal employers in their respective cities. There were, however, some important differences.

Company A was more innovative in its managerial practices. It was a family-owned company that valued its employees, gave them opportunities to grow in their jobs, and believed in participative management. Company B was more traditional and formal, maintained a strict hierarchy, and believed in management from the top down. However, Company B was just as willing as Company A to open its doors to the research, perhaps hoping to learn something that could help it deal with some of its problems. It was a basically solid company that was experiencing some employee discontent, and it was aware that it might need some revisions in its managerial practices. Company A was especially eager to have the information the research might produce, since it prided itself on being willing to learn and improve, no matter how well things were going. It also might be important to note that Company A was eighty years old, while Company B was only half that age.

Composition of Samples. A sample of 418 was obtained from Company A and 430 from Company B, representing roughly 70 percent of the total number of employees in each company.

Age distribution. The age distribution of both companies was similar. The average age of employees was about 35 and the age range covered the early 20s (with a small number under 20) all the way up to typical retirement age, 60 to 65. From previous research, as well as deductive reasoning, it is hypothesized that employee age will correlate positively with level of commitment to the organization, but not necessarily with the level of commitment to the work or co-workers.

Tenure (years with the company). There were some interesting differences in the distribution of years with the company. The average for Company A was about 9 and for Company B was about 5, which is consistent with the respective life spans of each company, but the distributions were very different. At Company B, 37 percent of the sample were people who had been hired within the last two years, compared with 24 percent in Company A. Company B had a major hiring period in the late 1970s, which was also the case for Company A, but not nearly to the same extent.

Based upon previous research, it is hypothesized that the number of years of employment at the organization will correlate positively with the level of commitment to the organization, but not necessarily with the level of commitment to the work or co-workers.

Gender. There were differences in gender distribution at the two companies. In the sample from Company A, 72 percent were men; in Company B's sample, 81 percent were men. It was not possible to determine what accounted for this difference, but a likely factor may have been a more limited labor market available to Company A, which might have resulted in greater employment opportunities for women in an industry that usually is male dominated. The distribution of men and women in both companies showed a disproportionate percentage of women in the lower ranks, but the pattern was more severe at Company A than at Company B. Again, no clear explanation can be offered, but the disparity could have been related to a number of factors. Management practices were likely to be one factor, but since the pattern was more pronounced at Company A, whose organizational qualities, as Dr. Herman found, were the more enlightened, it seems reasonable to conclude that the employment needs of Company A were at operational levels and being filled by the available labor pool, which included large numbers of women. On the basis of previous research, it is hypothesized that female employees will show significantly higher levels of commitment than male employees in one or more of the categories.

Position (level) in the company. The samples included all levels of the organization, except senior executives. In the Company A sample, 168 employees were salaried (most in managerial positions) and 238 were hourly (technical and support services). Twelve were in special contract roles and could not be classified as either salaried or hourly. In Company B, 157 employees in the sample were salaried, 261 were hourly, and 12 were not classifiable.

Based upon previous research and the increasing degree of self-management related to organizational level, it is hypothesized that the level of the employee in the organization will correlate positively with commitment to the work and to the organization, but not necessarily to co-workers.

Educational level. The two companies were very different with respect to educational levels. In the sample from Company A, 48 percent had not gone beyond high school and 52 percent had at least some post-secondary education; the vast majority of the larger group had graduated from college or technical school. In the Company B sample, 35 percent had no more than a high school education, while 65 percent had gone beyond high school, most completing at least college or technical school. Also of particular note was that in Company A only 3 percent had advanced degrees (masters or doctoral), while in the Company B sample 6 percent had advanced degrees. One likely explanation for the fact that Company B had a more highly educated population of employees than Company A was the difference in the ages of the companies. As is the case in most promote-from-within organizations, the people who have moved up through the ranks tend to be the people who have been around for many years and, compared with more recent hires, their levels of education are likely to be somewhat lower. Furthermore, as already noted, the average tenure at Company B was shorter than that at Company A; consequently, the hiring burst of the late 1970s likely filled Company B's ranks, even at the lower levels of a high tech company, with people who had some education beyond high school.

Additional demographic data. Some additional demographic information was obtained, more to provide a richer picture of each sample than to test any hypothesized relationships to commitment scores. This information included:

- Marital status
- Whether they had school-age children
- Distance from home to work

In Company A, 29 percent were single or divorced, 71 percent were married; in Company B 32 percent were single or divorced, while 68 percent were married. The differences between the companies were consistent with the age differences. In Company A, 43 percent had school-age children; 57 percent did not. In Company B, 36 percent had school-age children, while 64 percent did not. Evidently, there were more single parents with school-age children in Company A than in Company B, which might relate to the greater number of women employed at Company A.

The differences in commuting distances for the two companies were considerable. At Company A, 78 percent of the employees lived within 10 miles of the plant, while at Company B only 43 percent lived that close. At Company A, 18 percent lived 10 to 25 miles from the plant and only 4 percent lived farther away than that. At Company B, 38 percent lived 10 to 25 miles from the plant, but 19 percent lived farther away. The differences in distance from work related directly to their geographic situations. Company B was located in a city at least 10 times the size of the one in which Company A was located, which produced a much larger geographic dispersion of employees for Company B.

Other Variables. Information that had direct relevance to employee commitment, in addition to those research variables already covered, (age, years with company, gender, level in the organization, and educational level) were:

- Whether the employee had job training
- Desire or lack of desire for more responsibility
- Success or lack of success in achieving goals
- Expectations about reaching future goals
- Performance levels

Previous job training. Data on job training were available from Company B only. Most of the training was in technical skills as opposed to management skills. However, since the provision of training can, among other things, represent a commitment on the part of an organization to employee development, it is hypthesized that employees who received training will show higher levels of commitment to the work and the organization, but not necessarily to co-workers, than those who did not receive training.

It might also be argued in support of this hypothesis that the selection of those to be trained is likely to favor employees who already have demonstrated commitment to their jobs.

Desire for greater responsibility. On this variable the two companies were similar. At Company A, 80 percent reported that they desired more responsibility; at Company B the figure was 84 percent.

This is a difficult item to interpret, because a desire for more responsibility might reflect previous positive experience with responsibility or frustration from not having had it. Since the desire for it was slightly higher at Company B, which had some problems in its management practices, it seems logical to assume that frustration was behind at least some of the desire for more responsibility. In other words, the fact that B was a company with a higher percentage of younger, more recently hired employees than A would suggest that the desire for participation in decision-making would be relatively strong. Since the company tended to be fairly traditional and hierarchical in its policies, the frustration level related to participation in decision-making responsibility also was likely to be strong.

How desire for more responsibility might relate to commitment is an empirical question. It could be argued that not having the level of responsibility one desires tends to lower one's level of commitment, at least to the organization; it also could be argued that those who are most committed are those who will seek increased levels of responsibility. Given both arguments, no specific hypothesis can be offered.

Goal achievement. It is probably an established fact that success or failure in achieving one's goals has a powerful effect on one's attitude and feeling about work and perhaps about the setting in which that work is conducted. Whether we use reinforcement theory or expectancy theory to explain this phenomenon is not important here. What is important is that this variable provides one link between the reward system and commitment. Furthermore, goal achievement tends to affect a person's subsequent expectations about reaching future goals, which may be the more significant relationship in an employee's level of commitment, at least to the work and probably to the organization. At Company A, 19 percent of the sample reported that they had reached their career goals at the company; at Company B, 17 percent reported having reached career goals.

It turned out that using the word *career* in the question raised some difficulties in interpreting these figures and, consequently, any findings related to this factor. The group that reported having reached its career goals was likely to have included those nearing the ends of their careers. However, it was unclear how others in the sample might have interpreted the question. If they assumed that it was intended to reflect the degree to which a person is experiencing success in achieving career goals, they might have answered affirmatively, even though they had not yet fully attained their career goals. On the other hand, if they assumed that the question pertained to the end point of a career at the company, a negative response might have been appropriate for those who were experiencing success, but were still at some career midpoint. Their negative responses would not distinguish them from those who answered "no" because they had, in fact, been experiencing little or no success at the company. This sounds complicated, but one can appreciate the ambiguity created by the language in the item. Given these complexities and ambiguities, no hypothsis is offered for the relationship between goal achievement and commitment.

Expectations for goal achievement. With respect to the employee's expectation of success in attaining future goals at the company, the picture was less ambiguous. At Company A, 75 percent indicated a positive expectation and at Company B only 50 percent had a positive expectation, reflecting a potentially serious morale problem at Company B. This was consistent with the qualitative picture presented in Dr. Herman's research and will be discussed later in this chapter. Previous research, as well as the conceptual model covered in Chapter 2, support a hypothesis that employees with positive expectations regarding goal achievement will show higher levels of commitment to their work and to the organization, but not necessarily to co-workers, than will employees with negative expectations.

Performance ratings. The measures of performance in the two companies were different in at least two important respects. Company A used a five-level system and Company B used a four-level system. This difference, of course, affected the statistical results and required some structuring of the data to allow for useful comparisons of the companies in the relationship between CDI scores and performance ratings. Also, Company A had no restrictions on or requirements for the distribution of employees among the five levels; Company B used a forced distribution, limiting the number of ratings that could fall into a given category. This policy was implemented at departmental levels, thus requiring managers, irrespective of the size of the department, to force the ratings into compliance with the limits. Although it was difficult to know exactly how this situation at Company B would affect employee commitment, it was not unreasonable to expect that the effect was likely to be negative, at least in comparison with Company A's situation. It was also likely to distort the relationships obtained between commitment and performance because an unknown percentage of high performing employees may have been forced into a lower category, and vice versa for some percentage of low performing employees. Considering the many differences between the companies in their respective management practices and philosophies, one cannot determine the specific effect of the performance appraisal policy.

Table 4.2
Distributions of Performance Ratings

Company A		Company B	
Rating	Frequency	Rating	Frequency
1. Superior	64	1. Outstanding	71
2. Better than average	197	2. Superior	134
3. Average	105	3. Competent	140
4. Below average	18	4. Weak	11
5. Poor	4		

Table 4.2 shows the numbers of employees who fell into the five perform-ance levels in the Company A sample and into the four levels in the Company B sample. It is important to note the apparent effect of the forced distribution in Company B's sample. Although there was some tendency for the ratings to be biased in a positive direction (58 percent in the upper two categories), the picture was much more balanced than in Company A, which showed a strong positive bias (67 percent in the top two categories and 33 percent in the lower three). It was apparent that the middle category at Company A, which was identified as "average," was, in fact, below average for the com-pany. Since there was no way to know how the choice of terminology, which clearly was different for the two companies, might affect the ratings, it was necessary to take the numerical designations at face value.

With respect to both companies it is hypothesized that employee perform-ance will correlate positively with the level of commitment to the work, co-workers, and the organization.

An Overview of the Two Companies

In Dr. Herman's research the qualitative contrast between the two organ-izations was distinct. She found Company A to be what she called "high-spirited." Despite slow economic times and the strain on company resources, the employees at Company A valued the quality of life there and the level of respect with which they were treated by management. The employees felt "proud of A's reputation as an excellent place to work." As one employee put it, "I would say 75 to 80 percent of the people either are excited about being here or have the potential to be excited about being here." The overall management style at Company A was participative, communication was open, and employees were given a great deal of responsibility and personal latitude to manage themselves individually and as teams. Although there were many employees who reported dissatisfaction with management policies, some aspects of the compensation system, and the presence of some "deaf ears" at the top, the comments in Dr. Herman's data were positive overall and reflected an organization with good management practices and a well-conceived reward system. Relationships among employees were described as collaborative.

The story at Company B was quite different. There were a number of employees who believed in the company and still felt some positive company spirit. There also were many employees who felt that the company still offered "challenging, exciting, interesting opportunities at all levels of the company." However, a large percentage reported feeling that the organization failed to respect, appreciate, trust, listen to, or value them. This seemed to be the case at all levels and divisions of the system. The structure was formal and more hierarchical than at Company A, and control was exercised from the top down through close supervision. Employees reported inequities in the reward system and inconsistencies in the application of rules and discipline. The atmosphere was described as tense and laden with problems, and internal relationships were described as highly competitive.

The differences between A and B provided a natural experiment for this research. In addition to being able to cross-validate any empirical relationships obtained between commitment scores and other variables, it also was possible to test the sensitivity of the commitment measures to differences in overall organizational cultures, at least insofar as they were reflected in Dr. Herman's qualitative data.

The hypothesis here is that Company A will show significantly higher levels of commitment to the work and the organization, but not necessarily to co-workers, than will Company B.

Chapter 5

What the Study Produced

The research data are intended to serve two purposes. One is to establish a normative base, or at least the first stage of one, for comparing CDI scores obtained for diagnosis and application. The second relates directly to the research questions and hypotheses generated from previous research. The analyses were conducted for Company A and Company B separately. The normative data are presented in Appendix A rather than in the body of this chapter because those data are relevant primarily for users of the CDI. Also, for the comparisons of Companies A and B, only the results of the statistical tests are reported in this chapter; the distributions of scores for each company in each commitment category are presented in Appendix A.

Before proceeding with the the results of the research, I think it is important to set the stage. For those not familiar with statistical methods, or who have long since forgotten what they once learned, Appendix B provides a brief introduction and review of the basic statistical methods used to analyze the data. It might be useful to read that section before continuing with this chapter. As it turns out, most of the analysis is fairly straightforward and involves easily understood concepts.

Research Findings

This section looks briefly (Chapter 6 is devoted to a detailed discussion) at the results obtained from the CDI data for each company relative to:

- Age
- Years at the company
- Gender
- Position (level) in the company
- Education
- Job training
- Desire for greater job responsibility
- Goal achievement
- Expectations about goal achievement
- Performance ratings

Age and Commitment

Similar patterns were found in the two companies with respect to the relationship between age and commitment scores. Table 5.1 shows the correlation coefficients for both companies in each of the categories and for the total CDI scores.

The data indicate that older employees tend to be more committed than younger workers to their work and the organization, but apparently not to their co-workers.

Tenure and Commitment

As shown in Table 5.2, the results for tenure and commitment from the two companies were similar, with the one exception: the significant correlation between years at the company and commitment to the organization for Company B.

Although it is not a very strong relationship, it is interesting to note that it occurs in the younger of the two companies and in the one whose management practices were the more traditional.

Gender and Commitment

Although the general direction of the differences between male and female employees is similar in the two companies, the figures in Table 5.3 show that the differences between the means for each gender are clearly stronger at Company A than at Company B.

Table 5.1
Age and Commitment Correlations

Dimension	Company A	Company B
Work	r = .21 (p<.01)	r = .27 (p<.01)
Co-worker	r = .05 (ns)*	r = .06 (ns)
Organization	r = .20 (p<.01)	r = .25 (p<.01)
Total score	r = .20 (p<.01)	r = .24 (p<.01)

* The abbreviation (ns) is used in all tables to indicate that a given statistic is "not significant," i.e., that it could have occurred by chance more than one time (p>.01) or more than five times (p>.05) in a hundred.

The overall pattern from the two companies reflects higher commitment scores from women than men. The differences were statistically significant for two of the three dimensions and for the total at Company A, but significant only for commitment to co-workers at Company B. The strongest difference at Company A was for co-worker commitment.

Table 5.2
Years at Company and Commitment Correlations

	Company A	Company B
Work	r = .03 (ns)	r = .06 (ns)
Co-worker	r = .05 (ns)	r = .03 (ns)
Organization	r = .04 (ns)	r = .14 (p<.01)
Total score	r = .01 (ns)	r = .09 (ns)

Table 5.3
Gender and Commitment Means

Company A			
Dimension	Male Mean	Female Mean	Significance of Difference
Work	40.3	42.5	p<.05
Co-worker	36.4	38.8	p<.01
Organization	39.0	40.7	ns
Total score	115.7	122.3	p<.01
Company B			
Work	39.0	38.9	ns
Co-worker	38.1	39.9	p<.05
Organization	34.7	36.1	ns
Total score	111.9	114.9	ns

Position and Commitment

These results clearly support the hypothesis for position and commitment, but with one modification referring to commitment to co-workers. As shown in Table 5.4, position in the company correlates significantly with level of commitment in all categories for both companies.

One striking result is the correlation in Company B between position in the company and level of commitment to the organization. It is twice that of the other two categories for Company B and considerably higher than any of the figures for Company A. This will merit some attention in the next chapter.

Educational Level and Commitment

With respect to educational level we find a contrast between the two companies. The figures in Table 5.5 show that in Company A, education clearly is a significant factor relative to all three categories of commitment; in Company B it is not, with the possible exception of a very low correlation between educational level and commitment to the organization.

Job Training and Commitment

The data on job training and commitment were obtained at Company B only. Table 5.6 shows the means for the two groupings, those who did and those who did not have job training, for each of the commitment dimensions.

The strongest relationship between commitment and job training occurs for organizational commitment, with commitment to work a close second. Evidently, co-worker commitment is not affected by, nor does it affect, whether the employee received training.

Desire for Greater Responsibility and Commitment

Responsibility and commitment provide another interesting contrast between the two companies. In this instance Company B's results show this variable to be important in relation to employee commitment, whereas Company A's data do not, except for the organization dimension. The results appear in Table 5.7.

Clearly, the reasons that employees did or did not seek greater responsibility were different at the two companies, and the importance of commitment relative to desire for more responsibility was greater at Company B than at Company A.

Table 5.4
Position Level and Commitment Correlations

	Company A	Company B
Work	r = .19 (p<.01)	r = .17 (p<.01)
Co-worker	r = .22 (p<.01)	r = .16 (p<.01)
Organization	r = .24 (p<.01)	r = .34 (p<.01)
Total score	r = .27 (p<.01)	r = .27 (p<.01)

Table 5.5
Education and Commitment Correlations

Dimension	Company A	Company B
Work	r = .17 (p<.01)	r = .02 (ns)
Co-worker	r = .19 (p<.01)	r = .08 (ns)
Organization	r = .21 (p<.01)	r = .12 (p<.05)
Total score	r = .23 (p<.01)	r = .09 (ns)

Table 5.6
Job Training and Commitment Means

Dimension	Mean of Those With Training	Mean of Those Without Training	Significance of Difference
Work	40.2	38.2	p< .05
Co-worker	39.1	38.1	ns
Organization	36.5	34.1	p< .01
Total score	115.8	110.4	p< .01

Table 5.7

Mean Scores for Desire for More Responsibility and Commitment

Dimension	Mean of Those Seeking More Responsibility	Mean of Those Not Seeking More Responsibility	Significance of Difference
Company A			
Work	40.4	39.9	ns
Co-worker	37.2	36.4	ns
Organization	39.5	37.3	p<.05
Total score	117.1	114.4	ns
Company B			
Work	39.7	37.3	p<.05
Co-workers	39.1	35.0	p<.01
Organization	35.9	31.8	p<.01
Total score	114.7	104.0	p<.01

Goal Achievement and Commitment

The two companies were almost identical in the percentages of employees who reported that they had reached their career goals. In Company A, 19 percent reported that they had; at Company B the figure was 18 percent. There is nothing surprising or unusual about these figures, because one would expect that many working people continue to work in part to achieve career goals. Those who reported that they had reached their goals were either close to retirement or in the wrong career tracks, or may have found the question personally irrelevant. It turned out that there were no significant differences between the two groups at either company.

Expectations for Goal Achievement and Commitment

Expectations turned out to be an important set of findings, especially in relation to the conceptual model discussed in Chapter 2. Table 5.8 shows

Table 5.8
Mean Scores for Expectations for Goal Achievement and Commitment

Dimension	Mean of Those with Positive Expectation	Mean of Those with Negative Expectation	Significance of Difference
Company A			
Work	41.6	37.2	p<.01
Co-worker	37.9	34.5	p<.01
Organization	41.3	33.4	p<.01
Total score	120.8	105.1	p<.01
Company B			
Work	41.0	36.6	p<.01
Co-worker	39.8	37.0	p<.01
Organization	37.8	31.9	p<.01
Total score	118.8	105.5	p<.01

that in both companies those employees who stated that they expected to achieve their goals, compared with those who stated the opposite, had significantly higher commitment scores in all categories.

Performance Ratings and Commitment

It should be kept in mind that the measures of performance are inherently subjective, although both companies had fairly elaborate procedures for documenting each employee's performance. As with most performance appraisal systems, the procedures for managers tended to be even more subjective than those for operational employees, since the work of the latter is more directly measurable.

In examining the correlations between CDI scores and performance ratings I decided to use two different groupings of data. The first step was to compute the correlations for each company as a whole; the next step required

Table 5.9
Performance and Commitment Correlations for Each Company

Dimension	Company A	Company B
Work	r = .30 (p<.01)	r = .14 (p<.01)
Co-worker	r = .19 (p<.01)	r = .23 (p<.01)
Organization	r = .35 (p<.01)	r = .15 (p<.01)
Total Score	r = .35 (p<.01)	r = .20 (p<.01)

Table 5.10
Performance and Commitment Correlations for Managers and Operational
Employees Separately in Each Company

	Company A	
Dimension	Management	Operational
	(n = 168)	(n = 238)
Work	r = .18 (p<.05)	r = .35 (p<.01)
Co-worker	r = .18 (p<.05)	r = .15 (p<.05)
Organization	r = .28 (p<.01)	r = .38 (p<.01)
Total score	r = .28 (p<.01)	r = .37 (p<.01)

	Company B	
Dimension	Management	Operational
	(n = 158)	(n = 262)
Work	r = .14 (p<.05)	r = .15 (p<.05)
Co-worker	r = .20 (p<.01)	r = .22 (p<.01)
Organization	r = .17 (p<.05)	r = .08 (ns)
Total score	r = .21 (p<.01)	r = .17 (p<.05)

separating the samples in each company into two groupings, management and operational employees, then computing the correlations for those groups independently. The second step was necessary because of the significant correlation between position in the company and commitment scores at both companies and in all categories. The second analysis was intended to test the degree to which performance correlates with commitment, irrespective of position. Table 5.9 shows the first set of figures: those from each company as a whole. Table 5.10 shows the correlations for managers and for hourly employees separately.

It should be noted that because the sample sizes for these correlations were smaller than those in Table 5.9, the correlation coefficients had to be greater in order to attain significance. For example, the correlation of 0.14 in Table 5.9 is significant at a 1 percent confidence level; the same figure in Table 5.10 is significant at only the 5 percent level of confidence.

Comparisons of the Two Companies

The comparisons of the companies were conducted with total company data and then with data for the management and operational levels. The total sample for Company A was 418; the sample sizes for management and operational were 168 and 238, respectively, with 12 employees not classifiable in either group. The total sample for Company B was 430; the sample sizes for management and operational were 157 and 261, respectively, with 12 employees not classifiable. It is important to note that the smaller samples involved in the comparisons of the subgroups made the statistical tests less sensitive to differences than was the case for the total company samples.

Tables 5.11 through 5.13 show the results of the comparisons for the total samples (Table 5.11), for the management samples (Table 5.12), and for the hourly worker samples (Table 5.13).

The most striking result is the significance of the differences in the means for the commitment-to-organization category, which were significant in all three groupings of the data. This finding merits considerable discussion in Chapter 6.

These results provide a much clearer differentiation between the two companies with respect to their relative levels of commitment. The significant difference between the means of the total CDI scores was determined mostly by the organizational commitment factor. The employees' level of commitment to the organization turned out to be more sensitive than the commitment levels in the other two categories to the effect of the different management practices at the two companies. This finding will be discussed further in the next chapter.

Table 5.11
Commitment Means for Total Samples in Companies A and B

Dimension	Company A	Company B	Significance of Difference
Work	40.5	38.9	n.s.
Co-worker	37.0	38.0	n.s.
Organization	39.0	35.0	p<.01
Total score	116.8	112.2	p<.01

Table 5.12
Commitment Means for Management Samples in Companies A and B

Dimension	Company A	Company B	Significance of Difference
Work	42.5	41.0	ns
Co-worker	39.1	39.9	ns
Organization	42.1	38.7	p<.01
Total score	123.8	119.6	ns

Table 5.13
Commitment Means for Operational Employee Samples in Companies A and B

Dimension	Company A	Company B	Significance of Difference
Work	38.9	37.8	ns
Co-worker	35.7	37.8	ns
Organization	36.9	33.0	p<.01
Total score	111.5	109.6	ns

Table 5.14

Correlations among Age, Years at Company, Level in Company, and Educational Level

Dimensions	Company A	Company B
Age & tenure	r = .62 (p<.01)	r = .43 (p<.01)
Age & position	r = .08 (ns)	r = .25 (p<.01)
Age & educational level	r = .12 (p<.05)	r = -.12 (p<.05)
Tenure & position	r = .09 (ns)	r = .30 (p<.01)
Tenure & educational level	r = -.19 (p<.01)	r = -.18 (p<.01)
Position & educational level	r = .59 (p<.01)	r = .33 (p<.01)

Relationships of Age, Tenure, Position, and Education

Several variables were interrelated and seemed to form a constellation of relationships. These included age, years with the company (tenure), level in the company (position) and level of education. The findings are shown in Table 5.14.

Chapter 6 discusses all the findings in detail, relating them to the theoretical concepts and to practical implications. That chapter begins with a brief summary of all the findings reported here.

What the Research Revealed

This chapter discusses the findings reported in Chapter 5 in both theoretical and practical terms. The distributions of scores for the various categories in the samples studied have more practical use than theoretical meaning (see Appendix A). They provide normative standards for judging individual, co-worker, and organizational scores obtained by users of the CDI. The correlations between CDI scores and other variables, as well as the differences in CDI scores between various groupings of the data, provide some practical guidelines for users and add to our understanding of the concept of commitment in organizations today. A summary of the findings, without statistical figures, is presented here, followed by a discussion.

Summary of Results

Age

In both companies, there was significant correlation between age and commitment to work and to the organization, but not with commitment to co-workers. The correlation between age and total score was also significant in both firms.

Tenure

The only significant correlation between commitment and years with the organization occurred at Company A in the category of organizational commitment.

Gender

At Company A women had significantly higher scores than men in commitment to work and co-workers, as well as total scores, but not in commitment to the organization. At Company B women had significantly higher commitment scores in co-worker commitment, but not in any other area or in total scores. It also should be noted that at Company A the differences between men and women for co-worker commitment were greater than the differences for commitment to work.

Position in the Company

In both companies the commitment scores correlated significantly with the employee's level in the organization in all categories and for the total score: the higher the level, the higher the commitment score. The strongest relationship was in the organizational commitment category at Company B.

Educational Level

At Company A educational level correlated significantly with commitment scores in all categories, as well as with the total scores. At Company B the only significant correlation—and it was a very low figure—was in the organizational category.

Job Training

The factor of job training was studied at Company B only. Those who had training showed commitment scores significantly higher in two categories than those who did not have training: commitment to the work and the organization, but not for commitment to co-workers.

Desire for Greater Responsibility

Some important differences between the companies were found in relation to desire for greater responsibility. At Company A those who desired more responsibility had significantly higher organizational commitment scores than those who did not desire more responsibility, but the differences in scores for the other categories were not significant. At Company B those who desired more responsibility had scores significantly higher (in all categories, including total score) than those who did not desire more responsibility.

Goal Achievement

There were no significant differences in commitment scores between those who reported they had and those who reported they had not reached their individual goals in their jobs at either company.

Expectations for Goal Achievement

In both companies expectations proved to be an important variable. The commitment scores for those employees who expressed positive expectations for reaching their career goals at the company were significantly higher in all categories than those same scores for employees with negative expectations.

Performance Ratings

In both companies there was significant correlation between employee performance ratings and commitment scores in all categories, but the correlations were much higher in Company A than in Company B. The correlations between performance and commitment for managers and operational employees grouped separately were significant in all categories for both companies, with one exception. The relationship was not significant for operational employees of Company B in the organizational commitment category. At Company A the correlations overall were much higher for the operational people than for the management group.

Comparing the Companies

The commitment scores for Company A were significantly higher than those for Company B in the category of organizational commitment and for the total scores. The differences were not significant for the work and co-worker categories, but the mean commitment score in the co-worker area was higher in Company B than in Company A. Additional comparisons separating management from hourly employees showed even greater differences between the companies in the organizational category, where the scores for Company B were the lowest.

Relationships of Age, Tenure, Position, and Education

Age, tenure, position, and education were interrelated to varying degrees at both companies. Age and years with the company were very strongly related, and position in the company correlated with both age and years with the company, as one would expect. Similarly, there was a high correlation between educational level and position in the organization. While the relationship was slight, but significant, educational level did correlate negatively with years at the company, suggesting that the most recent hires were among the better educated employees and probably were hired mostly into advanced technical positions. Since this was true for both companies, it probably reflects what occurred in many high tech organizations during the last decade.

The two very high correlations in Company A (age with tenure and position with education) suggest that employees stay with the company for a long time, but their tenure has little to do with their position in the organization, which is determined more by education than anything else. This is only partially true for Company B, where both age and years with the company are related to position in the organization.

Discussion of Results

Commitment and Age

The fact that age correlated positively with commitment to work and organization, but not with commitment to co-workers is important. Since these relationships were independent of years with the company (which did not correlate at all with commitment), I would suggest that some societal factor was operating that reflects generational differences, especially since it occurred in both companies. The more senior employees may have different expectations for their work lives than their younger counterparts. They may have a stronger set of values about pride in their work and in their organization, along with a strong orientation toward individual, rather than group, effort.

Commitment and Tenure

The puzzling part of the picture is that while the older employees were also those who had been with the companies the longest, there was virtually no correlation between tenure and commitment at either organization. One key factor might be position in the company. Most of the company veterans were still in the lower levels of the organizations at the time of the research, while many members of management, while older in years than the average employee, had been with the company for a relatively short time. These were the people who were hired into advanced positions because of their particular expertise and educational backgrounds. This overall pattern easily could have canceled the correlation expected between commitment and tenure.

Another explanation for this pattern may be that commitment, if it develops, does so within the first few years of employment and levels off from there. Consequently, the wide range of years of employment that existed in both samples is not relevant as a test of commitment over time. A better test of the relationship would have to involve studying a sample of newly hired employees over a period of months or, at most, the first few years of their employment. My experience in consulting to a number of different organizations fits the latter thesis, since many companies report the first two to three years as critical in determining whether an employee will stay with or leave the company.

Commitment and Gender

The fact that women showed a higher level of commitment to co-workers than did men, while not surprising, is important, especially coming from two organizations that are decidedly male dominated. Given the direction many organizations are taking today (team-centered management), the fact that women tend to develop stronger identification with their co-workers than men suggests that team leadership in the future might be more suited to women than to men.

This is not to suggest that men are not suited to team leadership nor incapable of learning the requisite skills; that assertion would fly in the face of many years of experience in training both men and women for group leadership roles. It is only to suggest that any organization that has norms and customs that prevent women from entering positions of team leadership is not only blocking off the special abilities of women, but also is cheating the organization of a valuable resource.

In *Megatrends 2000,* Naisbitt and Aburdene suggest that the 1990s will be the "decade of women in leadership" (1990). In her 1990 article in the *Harvard Business Review,* Judy Rosener discusses how women's style of leadership tends to be more interactive than men's and more naturally suited to the team focus that future leadership roles will demand. Since not all women demonstrate strong interpersonal commitment, just as not all men demonstrate weak interpersonal commitment, it can be important for any organization moving toward a team approach to be capable of identifying those employees who have high potential for leadership roles, irrespective of gender or any other background factor. However, I suspect that over the long run the most effective team-centered organizations will have a substantial number of women as team leaders, hopefully at all levels of the system.

To accomplish these ends a company will have to pay careful attention to its management practices, especially its structure. In both companies studied there was a disproportionate number of women in the lower ranks, given the overall male-female balance in each company. No women occupied positions among the top officer ranks of either company. This may very well explain why despite their greater commitment to co-workers, the female employees in both companies did not show levels of commitment to work or the organization that were any higher than those of the men. I would hypothesize that if either company were to change its management practices in ways that brought more women into the upper ranks, the women's levels of commitment might be higher than those of the men in all categories.

With respect to structure, Sally Helgesen suggests in *The Female Advantage* (1990) that a "web" may be the most natural form for women, with leadership coming from the center rather than from the top, as in a hierarchy. She states that "the web facilitates direct communication, free-flowing and loosely structured, by providing points of contact and direct tangents along which to connect" (p. 50).

It may be a long time before we see many webs or networks appearing, which may pose some serious problems for women in leadership positions. However, the changes that are occurring in information technology are driving organizational structures in the same direction. Since webs or networks do seem to be more flexible and responsive to change, it seems inevitable that hierarchy eventually will be replaced, or at least seriously modified.

Commitment and Position in the Company

What seems eminently logical is the connection between position and level of commitment. People in higher levels of a company have jobs that are more varied, hold greater responsibility and autonomy, are more challenging, and in general are more intrinsically rewarding than the jobs at lower levels. Certainly there are important exceptions, especially in high tech organizations, but the general pattern is probably true. Consequently, we would expect to find a stronger identification with one's work and the organization at upper versus lower levels of a company.

I suspect that this difference will always exist, given the inherent nature of work in the higher positions of an organization. However, it does not preclude the opportunity to increase commitment levels for all employees, irrespective of their positions. One of the interesting findings was the very high correlation at Company B between position and commitment to the organization. I believe it reflects the strongly differentiated hierarchy in Company B in contrast to the more open system at Company A. The rise to the top in a strong hierarchy usually depends upon a willingness to accept the rules. To the extent that individuals actually come to identify with that system and work hard on its behalf, they can expect to advance to higher level positions. The formal organization of Company B is, therefore, more likely to foster the kind of commitment that reinforces a status hierarchy than would a more participative organization like Company A.

Commitment and Educational Level

The differences between the two companies with respect to the correlation between commitment and education can be attributed in part to a third factor, namely level (position) in the company. As reported earlier, the correlation between organizational level and commitment was significant for both companies. As it turns out, however, the correlation between position and educational level at Company A was 0.59 and only 0.33 at Company B. While both findings are significant, it is highly probable that education at Company

A is a greater differentiator of employee position than at Company B. The magnitude of the correlation at Company A suggests the presence of a strong common factor and also makes sense of the difference between the two companies.

A comparative analysis also shows the probable impact of Company B's hiring surge. The high percentage of recent hires in the sample from Company B, plus the fact that these were predominantly people with college and technical school degrees, suggests that either not enough time for enculturation had passed to allow for employee commitment to develop or that the management practices at Company B were such that a substantial percentage of the newly hired college and technical people were not identifying very strongly with their work, their co-workers, or with the organization. This is consistent with the explanation offered previously where it was suggested that the first few years seem to be critical in determining an employee's decision to remain with an organization.

Commitment and Job Training

Given the relationship between education and commitment, the strong correlation between job training and commitment is an especially important finding for Company B. The training programs there were almost all technical in nature, so the commitment scores make sense. The training, apart from any effect on skill level, clearly enhanced employee identification with the work, and apparently strengthened identification with the organization. I suspect that this occurred because the training helped employees see the connections between their jobs and overall company objectives (product and service). Because the training was not related to team building or group behavior, it is not surprising that no relationship was found between training and co-worker commitment.

It is unfortunate that similar data were not obtained from Company A, because that organization invested heavily in training programs of all kinds, including management and team leader skills.

Commitment and Desire for More Responsibility

The fact that a strong relationship was found between commitment and desire for more responsibility was not surprising, but the differences in the nature of that relationship at the two companies is especially important in light of their management practices.

The conclusion that the more committed employees in Company B were the ones who tended to desire greater responsibility makes sense and is certainly of importance to Company B. What does not seem to make sense is that this relationship did not also occur in Company A, which has the significantly higher levels of employee commitment. One would think that even among this group of employees, those who have the higher scores would also seek more responsibility in their jobs.

Furthermore, Company A, which already tended to give comparatively greater responsibility to employees, showed higher scores for commitment to the organization from those who desired more responsibility. In other words, those employees who were most strongly committed to the organization as a whole desired even greater responsibility than they already had, while differences in commitment to work and co-workers were unrelated to the desire for greater responsibility.

At Company B, which tends to exercise control from the top, all categories of commitment turned out to be predictive of the desire for greater responsibility. In short, despite its style of management, the most committed members of Company B still wished to take on more responsibility in their jobs. It is easy to see how a company like B could capitalize readily on its employees' commitment if it were to empower them and involve them more in running the organization.

Commitment and Goal Expectations

The results strongly confirmed the connection between an organization's reward system and the level of commitment of its employees. Which is cause and which is effect is impossible to determine, but, as suggested by the interactive model described in Chapter 2, these two sets of variables tend to be mutually reinforcing. Employees whose goal expectations are high tend to be those who are strongly committed. And that commitment evidently is not limited to just the work, but also pertains to relations with co-workers and to the organization overall.

When it comes to meeting goal expectations there was an important difference between the two companies, as described in Chapter 3: In Company A, 75 percent of the employees sampled stated that they did expect to achieve their career goals at the company; in Company B only 50 percent of the employees sampled stated that they expected to achieve their goals at the company.

These results demonstrate just how important it is for an organization's management practices to meet employees' expectations if the organization hopes to maintain and strengthen employees' commitment. Relative to Company A, Company B fell far short of engaging in such management practices. Even though, as pointed out in Chapter 2, goal attainment itself may not necessarily directly strengthen identification with work, co-worker, or the organization, it certainly helps to strengthen an employee's predisposition for putting forth a high level of effort to reach a given goal. This, in turn, reinforces the expectation that one can reach one's goals in the setting, which does then result in greater commitment. As the cycle continues and builds, a sense of intrinsic satisfaction develops with respect to the work and the context in which that work is carried out, including one's co-workers and the organization.

Commitment and Performance Ratings

In some respects we can consider employee performance to be the bottom line in this research. For most managers, whatever contributes to performance is what counts, whether it contributes directly, as might some technological change, or indirectly, as might some attitudinal change. In this case we can see that the following proposition holds true: the higher the level of employee commitment to work, co-worker, and organization, the higher the level of performance, at least insofar as the performance appraisal system validly reflects real performance.

The difference between the two companies in the strength of the correlation between commitment and performance is important. It may or may not reflect a real difference in the relationship between the two variables, but it is very likely that a significant aspect of the results pertain to differences in both the rating scales (five levels at Company A and four at Company B) and the procedure (Company B's use of a forced distribution, which was not used at Company A). The narrower the range of possible scores, the more a correlation figure will tend to underestimate the true relationship between two variables when each can be assumed to exist on a continuum. It is possible that the correlations between commitment and performance would have been similar had both companies been using comparable scales. Furthermore, it is likely that the correlations obtained from Company A are more accurate estimates of the true relationship between performance and commitment in general.

The pattern of correlations is worth examining. In Company A, apart from the relationship between total commitment scores and performance ($r = 0.35$), the strongest relationship was between organizational commitment and performance ($r = 0.35$), with commitment to work next ($r = 0.30$), and co-worker commitment lowest ($r = 0.19$). While all were, as reported, statistically significant, it is clear that co-worker commitment is a relatively weak predictor of employee performance in Company A.

By contrast, Company B's pattern was totally different and worthy of comment, despite the probable underestimations reflected in the figures. The strongest relationship was between commitment and performance in the co-worker category ($r = 0.23$), while both commitment to work and to the organization were relatively poor predictors of performance ($r = 0.14$ and 0.15, respectively). Evidently, in Company B co-worker commitment was a more significant predictor of performance than it was at Company A.

It also was a relatively stronger predictor of performance than any of the other commitment scores obtained at Company B.

Given the emphasis of performance appraisals on individual behavior, it is certainly to be expected that commitment to work and to the total organization would be good predictors of employee performance, while commitment to co-workers would not, except in those instances (all too rare) when a worker's contribution to the group or team is explicitly emphasized. Therefore, the results from Company A are not surprising. But what would explain the results from Company B? My own interpretation is that the evaluation method at Company B distorted any correlations with commitment to work and to the organization, resulting in a high percentage of false positives (poor performers who got pushed up into a higher level than they deserved) and false negatives (high performers who got pushed down to a level below that which truly reflected their performances). I also would expect that this outcome could produce some employee disenchantment with the whole appraisal system, since it is inevitably unfair to a certain percentage of employees who actually perform well but get squeezed out of available slots at the top.

This phenomenon reminds me of the effects of forced grade distributions in educational settings. While they may make inherent sense as a screening device in large introductory courses, they often are used inappropriately in smaller, more advanced courses where one would expect to find the better and more committed students. The result is that even quite satisfactory performance is assigned a very low grade because it happens to be lower (often by only a small margin) than that of the majority of the class. That usually leads to discouragement and a loss of commitment on the part of the student. Many managers I have known have had this experience, only to forget it when they set up a similar forced distribution for their employees, even though these employees may be among the best available.

In examining the results from the separate analyses of the managers and the operational employees, we see some very important phenomena. First of all, it is important that the correlations held up even after controlling for the effect of level in the company, which also correlated with commitment. Furthermore, this analysis revealed some patterns that apparently were masked by the analysis that combined both groupings.

It is really striking that in Company A, the strongest correlations between commitment and performance occurred in the operational group and by a substantial margin. What it says is that if that company wants to predict performance by knowing level of commitment, it can do a better job with the employees in the lower ranks of the organization than it can with managers. The organizational commitment scores for the managers at Company A did correlate significantly with the performance ratings, but the figure ($r = 0.28$) was substantially lower than that for the operational employees ($r = 0.38$).

Now, this may say something about the nature of the appraisal process used by Company A. It might reflect the possibility, or perhaps the likelihood, that those employees who have reached managerial positions tend to be the more committed individuals and would be less varied in their performance ratings; it could be due to the fact that performance appraisals usually are conducted by management, who would tend to be more discriminating with their hourly subordinates than they would be with other managers; or it could be some combination of both. The important thing in generalizing from these results is that an instrument or procedure (like the CDI) that is intended to predict subsequent behavior must be used cautiously, keeping in mind the various contingencies that might affect its validity.

In Company B the difference between management and operational employees was not very significant. However, there are two important features that stand out. One is that commitment to the organization correlated significantly with performance for managers, but not for hourlies; the other is that the correlations for the hourly employees of the two companies were completely different. Clearly, in Company A it can be useful to know the levels of operational employees' commitment in order to predict their levels of performance; in Company B it is not useful to have that information for predictive purposes, at least in relation to the type of performance measures that were used. Evidently, the combination of the forced distribution and narrow range of ratings at Company B resulted in the absence of a useful correlation between employee performance and level of commitment to the organization.

The Problem with Performance Appraisal

In reflecting on these results it struck me that neither company, and perhaps no major company, uses a performance appraisal system that emphasizes commitment. Every evaluation method I know of or have heard about places its emphasis on individual performance relative to external expectations. The best ones develop approaches that involve employees in the process of evaluation, negotiate performance expectations with the employees, occur frequently enough to generate useful corrective feedback, are interactive and share control of the process with the employees, emphasize learning, and are not punitive. However, they also tend to connect performance to external criteria, emphasize and reward individual effort, usually are not collaborative, and almost always give primary attention to measurable outcomes.

The typical system focuses either on some judgment about an employee's worth to the organization or on the development of the employee through feedback. Most use multiple standards, including quantity, quality, cooperation, dependability, attendance, and so on, and translate these standards into some rating form that is filled out by the supervisor or jointly by the employee and supervisor. The forms generally are structured as rating scales, with the various criteria listed on separate dimensions. Some attach differential weightings to the criteria, some use ranking methods, some include descriptive essays or critical examples to back up a rating, and many reduce all the data to a single, global judgment, as was the case with both companies used in the research. Many modern approaches to performance appraisal build on the management-by-objectives (MBO) concept, which involves having an employee and a supervisor jointly establish performance goals for the employee and then measure performance relative to the attainment of those goals.

By now one might wonder what there is to criticize in these principles. In terms of what organizations have sought traditionally, probably very little. But in terms of what many organizations are seeking now, there is much to be criticized, mainly that they do not foster identification with any aspect of the work experience. Instead, they foster compliance to the performance standards set by the organization. The locus of control remains in the system and/or with the supervisor and not with the individual or group. I have spoken with many human resources managers and have found very few who are really satisfied with their companies' performance evaluation systems, despite many years of careful design and experimentation. They all tell me that "something just isn't right with our approach," but they have not figured out what that is. What I would suggest is that even the best of the systems now in place may be working from the wrong premise for the direction the organization is taking. It can be stated that Companies A and B probably were working from a control or compliance mentality rather than a commitment mentality.

Edward Deming, the father of the total quality movement, advocates the elimination of performance evaluations altogether. He insists that they tend to "encourage short-term performance at the expense of long-term planning, . . . discourage risk-taking, build fear, undermine teamwork, and pit people against each other for the same rewards" (Walton 1986, p. 91). He also points out that most managers dread making these judgments.

What I suggest is not the elimination of performance appraisal, but approaching it from a commitment-based perspective. Let me spell this out and offer some guidelines for designing such a system.

Commitment-based Performance Appraisal

The first thing that must happen is to disconnect performance from extrinsic rewards. I realize that this is heresy, but I believe that it is crucial to the long-range success of a commitment-centered appraisal system. All evaluation must be tied to the work itself, to relationships with co-workers, and to strengthening organizational identification. When those outcomes occur, high performance will follow. It is similar to the position taken by Jan Carlzon, president of SAS, when he suggested that if you provide good customer service, the profits will eventually take care of themselves (Albrecht, 1988). My point is that we have been so concerned about measurable performance that we end up using control-centered evaluation methods even in a commitment-centered setting. The contradiction only hurts performance over the long term.

The second thing to do is eliminate all internal competition for rewards; create an environment in which all rewards are attained through collaborative effort. Individual recognition always must occur within the context of the team or the organization as a whole and must be related to the employee's contribution to overall effort. In Chapter 10 I describe in greater detail a team-centered approach to performance appraisal using peer evaluations, but at this point it is worth mentioning that the approach includes factors not directly related to productivity.

One of the serious problems inherent in the use of competitive, extrinsic incentives for performance is that they tend to undermine the basic purpose for which they are intended. A good example of this is the recent surge in interest in the Malcolm Baldridge Award on the part of major corporations. It is intended to symbolize the achievement of quality, not serve as an end in itself. However, it is easy for companies to become so obsessed with getting the award that they do not seem to care how much pressure they put on their employees. The result is that the quality of the work environment, which is part of what the award symbolizes, actually may go down in order to make the visible aspects of the company's quality (product or service) look good. Instead of creating a high commitment system, one truly committed to excellence, what results is a high compliance system in which management is overcontrolling its workers in order to get what, in fact, it probably would not deserve.

Let us look at each commitment category and see how performance can be defined in terms of that category.

Identification with Work. I suggest emphasizing the following five criteria for appraising employees' task-related efforts:

1. The extent to which individuals act autonomously (operate without dependence upon outside direction).
2. The extent to which individuals take responsibility for the completion of their own work.
3. The extent to which individuals take initiative in dealing with problems that arise unexpectedly.
4. The extent to which individuals learn from their mistakes and tend not to repeat them.
5. The extent to which individuals seek to strengthen their job knowledge and expertise in relation to any aspects of the work or the organization.

High performance in these five areas will tend to foster employees' identification with the work by increasing their ownership in how it is carried out. Furthermore, the work will become a natural context for personal learning and growth, and employees will develop internalized standards to guide future actions. Although the best source of data for this aspect of the appraisal is likely to be an employee's own co-workers, there may be sources of information in other parts of the organization, such as human resources personnel or members of the training staff.

For this aspect of the appraisal to work best and to foster individual commitment to the work, I would suggest allowing the employees to control the process to a substantial degree. This would be consistent with a commitment-based approach, which emphasizes the value of empowering employees.

Identification with Co-Workers (the Team). I suggest emphasizing the following five criteria for appraising an employee's performance relative to co-workers:

1. The individual's contribution to the team's *task* through a variety of roles or functions (to be discussed in Chapter 10).
2. The individual's contribution to team *maintenance* through a variety of roles or functions (to be discussed in Chapter 10).
3. The extent to which the individual effectively represents the team vis-à-vis other parts of the organization.
4. The extent to which the individual serves as a role model for other team members, especially new members.
5. The extent to which the individual is able to subordinate personal needs to the best interests of the team.

High performance relative to these five criteria will strengthen employees' identification with their co-workers because the intrinsic rewards for these social behaviors also are directly related to personal growth and development. An important, if not imperative, part of this approach is that the group or team must manage the appraisal process. Any interference from outside, especially from top management, can have a deleterious effect on group cohesiveness and can damage the relationship of the individual to the group. Although management might feel reluctant to give away that much control, it is necessary if management wants to build a high level of commitment to team performance. It also may be necessary at times for management to live with appraisal outcomes with which it does not agree; to override them would only move the organization toward being a compliance-centered system.

Identification with the Organization. I suggest emphasizing the following five criteria for appraising employee performance relative to the organization:

1. The extent to which the individual seeks to learn about the organization, its history, operations, and future plans.

2. The willingness of the individual to call attention to the problems and mistakes that surface at an organizational level, often despite fears of personal retribution.

3. The willingness of the individual to offer ideas for ways to improve the organization.

4. The extent to which the individual serves as an ambassador of the organization in outside activities.

5. The extent to which the individual seeks opportunities to serve on committees or task forces that deal with overall organizational issues.

These five areas of activity relate directly to organizational identification and, like the other two areas, produce the intrinsic rewards that promote personal learning and growth. Unlike the previous category, upper management is likely to have knowledge of and play a significant role in the individual's contributions. The team can be a source of data and opinion, but should not hold exclusive control over the appraisal process, since it clearly goes beyond team boundaries. One useful step might be to create an organization-wide task force that seeks and organizes information pertaining to employees' contributions to the total effort. Such a task force must maintain a broad perspective and needs to stress the importance of total system goals, not local interests, in evaluating people.

One of the difficulties posed by my suggestions is the matter of documentation. It is relatively easy to document performance when the standards are quantifiable; but none of the fifteen criteria I have suggested is quantifiable and almost all are inherently subjective, requiring some kind of judgment by those conducting the appraisal. Although I offer no simple solution to the problem, my own experience, and that of some of my colleagues, is that a form of periodic review that focuses on critical incidents and examples related to the different criteria can be very useful. Also, since many organizations are using peer review as part of the process, an employee's co-workers can be a rich source of information which, despite its inherent subjectivity, tends to provide some degree of objectivity: Any given judgment can be confirmed or disconfirmed through multiple sources.

Comparing the Companies

It was hypothesized, based upon the differences in management practices, that Company A would show significantly higher levels of commitment than Company B. The results supported this hypothesis for one of the three dimensions, commitment to the organization, but not for the others. Furthermore, the difference was more pronounced for operational employees than for management.

What these findings tell us is that the impact of managerial practices, at least those conducted by the companies studied, tends to be more evident in operational employees than in management people. This should be no surprise to anyone who understands the dynamics of a multilevel organization.

Since the power resides at the top, the degree to which lower level employees are empowered to manage themselves is always at the discretion of management. It would appear that Companies A and B, while engaging in very different management styles with respect to the empowerment of their hourly people, are not that different in the way management personnel are treated. The result is that the managers in both companies, while different in their levels of commitment (A being significantly higher than B), are not nearly as far apart as the operational employees.

An important lesson in this for managers is that employee commitment needs to be understood through the eyes of the employees. What may appear to a manager to be a practice that fosters commitment may not be from the perspective of an employee whose job entails little self-management. By the same token, those practices that may have a major positive effect on employees' commitment might represent to a manager a minor change with little impact.

For example, when flextime was introduced it was intended for those jobs that were hourly and required a time clock. The objective was to increase the flexibility of employees to manage their working hours in order to accommodate personal and family needs. What some organizations did was introduce flextime to management, where people were salaried, did not use time clocks, and already were responsible for managing their own hours. As one might surmise, while the effect of flextime on hourly employees generally was positive, the effect on managers ranged from irrelevant to negative.

Although the difference between the two companies in the category of co-worker commitment was not significant, the fact that it was in the unpredicted direction (Company B higher than Company A) is worth comment. My own interpretation is that the negative climate for employees at Company B tended to foster stronger social bonding than one might expect. It is similar to the concept of cohesiveness in the face of a common enemy. In her discussion of the climate at Company B, Dr. Herman alluded to a shared distrust of management among a large number of the employees. It also might be noted from her study that the atmosphere at Company A was not very team centered. The emphasis at the company tended to be on individual opportunities and performance. Consequently, the difference in the co-worker commitment scores between the two companies might be attributable as much to Company A's low encouragement of team behavior as to Company B's co-worker social bonding.

Chapter 7

Commitment and Organizational Development

Research data of the kind generated by the CDI can be a powerful tool for organizational change. Like any survey research method, it provides a mirror for the company, a way of looking at itself, diagnosing some of its problems, testing the impact of many of its actions, or just taking a snapshot of the present state of affairs.

The large size of the samples in each of the two companies (A and B) made it possible to use statistical tests as a means of identifying significant factors related to measures of employee commitment. Conclusions could be drawn and applied to the larger context, although these same conclusions could not always be applied to more specific instances, to individuals or to smaller parts of the system, except where the data analysis actually was applied to those cases.

For example, the finding that employees in the upper levels of an organization tended to show higher levels of commitment to their work than those in lower levels does not necessarily mean that one could be confident that specific individuals in lower levels will show low levels of commitment to their work. An intervention like job redesign might make sense for the jobs at the lower levels overall, but whether that same intervention would make sense in a specific case would require a deeper analysis at that level and of that individual.

However, if used properly, the CDI can be effective for organizational change at a departmental or team level. What it requires is a more clinical application of the instrument, including attention to the three scores and perhaps using an item-by-item analysis and discussion. The data alone do not produce change; the information that people derive from the data and the learning process that follows are what make a difference.

Some organizational development consultants have claimed that it almost does not matter exactly what data one gathers, as long as the data stimulate learning and development. I would not hold to that extreme a position, but I do want to emphasize that the interpretation and subsequent use of CDI measures by a group or any set of individuals should fit the situation and the cast of people involved.

In the remainder of this chapter we will look at the actual and potential uses of the CDI in both the larger organizational context and the smaller, more group-focused setting.

Diagnosis

There are two very general ways to use the CDI data in organizational diagnosis. One way is *normative,* which requires comparison with other samples which, in the cases of Companies A and B, were other companies. I have found that most organizations do want to know how they compare with other places, especially competitors. The other way to use the measures is more *developmental,* which requires a specification of some standards or levels that the company deems desirable and using them to guide improvement. In order to establish such standards it is helpful, if not essential, to have some normative data. Otherwise, what is determined to be a level of commitment to strive for could be arbitrary at best and unrealistic at worst. The data from within a given organization often are enough to determine what is possible.

For example, I have found that a set of scores that are consistently lower in one department compared to other departments in an organization can provide a useful index of a problem. In a sense, the organization can develop its own internal norms for comparison of one department or group to another. The developmental perspective also encourages a longitudinal approach, in which case the group creates its own standard by looking at changes in scores over time and not so much at scores obtained at a given time.

Most organizations today do not stop with normative comparisons, unless, of course, the data either confirm what the company believed in the first place or the picture generated is too threatening for the company to cope with, leading to some form of denial or minimization. A healthy organization, even in dealing with threatening information, will want to understand what is going on and take some corrective actions. Certainly knowing just how committed its employees are and to what are vital considerations for organizational success. Obtaining a general picture of the system overall and some snapshots of subparts of that system are important first steps to organizational improvement.

Feedback to the Companies Studied. Part of the original agreement that Dr. Herman had with each company included the promise of feedback of the relevant findings, including both the quantitative and qualitative data.

Although there was no expectation of any follow-up or organizational intervention, the management of each company felt that it might learn something useful. With this in mind the findings presented in Chapter 5 were organized for presentation as feedback. It was like holding up a mirror to show the company what it was saying about itself with respect to employee commitment.

The presentation included a report of significant statistical results, histograms to show the distributions of commitment scores in the different categories, and graphs that illustrated relationships among important variables. It also included some limited comparisons of each company with the other, maintaining absolute confidentiality. Wherever possible, the quantitative and qualitative results were used in a complementary manner to reinforce the validity of each. As one might expect, there were some aspects of the data that confirmed already-held beliefs about the company and some that came as a total surprise.

At Company A, because the data reflected a generally positive picture and the attitude of management was open to new information, the response was quite positive. Management showed an eagerness to explore the data even beyond what was presented, as well as an interest in hearing some recommendations for improving weak areas.

For example, the fact that employees at the lower levels exhibited lower levels of commitment than those at higher levels raised some concerns as to whether management could do a better job of involving employees in decisions and exploring ways to improve the methods by which the work was carried out. Management was surprised to learn that the women were more committed employees than the men, especially in the co-worker category. This, coupled with the fact that the overall company score on commitment to co-workers was the lowest of the three categories and lower than that same score for "the other company" (whose other commitment scores had been significantly lower), gave Company A pause to reflect on the role of women as potentially strong team players who had not been empowered adequately.

It also became clear that Company A had a long way to go to build teamwork at a group level and that, although management espoused a strong belief in a team effort, this was not occurring as it should.

At Company B the response was not as receptive, especially with respect to the comparison with Company A. However, despite attempts to explain away some of the unpleasant findings, it was obvious that there was enough validity in the combined quantitative and qualitative results that management had to take them seriously. The chief executive officer was most troubled by the data and requested some recommendations from Dr. Herman, who developed a proposal for a team-building effort that started with top management. The overall pattern of results at Company B suggested a long-term effort beyond team building at the top, including some work redesign and a more team-centered operating style throughout the company.

In the next section I illustrate the ways in which the CDI data can be used directly by a department or small group for the purposes of team building. Although the examples discussed do not include the top management group at Company B, the issues in the examples would probably be very similar to those at Company B.

Applications to Team Building

Two applications will be discussed. The first involves a department at a medium-sized bank and the other a top management group at a small manufacturing firm. In each case the CDI was used as one method of diagnosing the group's strengths and weaknesses in working as an effective team. The same definition of teamwork was used in each case. In effect, *teamwork* was defined as 'the ability of a group of individuals to recognize, appreciate, and reinforce each other's contributions to the group objectives, to act cooperatively, to establish norms that support both task and maintenance goals, and to be willing to allow group priorities to take precedence over individual priorities.' Implied in the definition is the assumption that all group members are ready to examine and renegotiate role expectations as necessary.

The Bank Department. As an example of an application of the CDI to team building we will look at a group of twenty middle managers (including six women) in the main office of a small New England bank. The principal objective of the team-building effort was to improve the communication and cooperation among these managers. The quality of customer service had been suffering for some time because information was falling through the cracks, resulting in frequent failures to provide satisfactory service to the bank's clientele. The specific issues for team building pertained to a lack of attention to the interdependence of the tasks and responsibilities of these managers and the absence of a clear set of common goals. The CDI was employed as one data-gathering technique that could shed some light on differences in the managers' identification with their work, each other, and the bank as a whole, particularly as those factors might affect the group's ability to operate as a team.

Category analysis. The first step involved examining the CDI scores in each category and comparing them with the sample of 325 managers from the two companies that generated the normative data. Although the major benefits of using the CDI at a group level usually derive from a more clinical analysis of the data, a comparison can help form a judgment about the general level of commitment in the group relative to some normative standard. Although the 325 managers in the sample worked in manufacturing, their responsibilities and their needs were not very different from managers in other settings. Also, as pointed out in Chapter 4, the items in the instrument are not industry-specific but pertain to generic organizational behavior.

The mean score for identification with work in the bank group was 46.2, several points higher than the 41.5 obtained from the normative sample. It also should be noted that nine of the twenty members of the group had scores above 46, which placed them in the upper 25 percent of the normative sample, while no one scored below 36, which is the cutoff point for the lowest 25 percent. Therefore, it may be said that as a group, these managers were highly committed to their work.

The mean score for identification with co-workers in the bank group was 42, a few points higher than normative mean of 39.5. In this instance five of the six women scored in the top 25 percent, which has a cutoff point of 44, and just one person scored below the cutoff point of 35 for the bottom 25 percent. One also might note that while the mean for work commitment fell in the top 25 percent of the norms, the mean for co-worker commitment fell well within the middle 50 percent range. Here it can be said that although the bank group's level of commitment to each other was at least as high as one would expect, it did not, except for the five women, come up to the level reflected in the work commitment scores, indicating room for improvement.

With respect to identification with the organization, the mean score for the bank group was 42, only slightly higher than the normative score of 40.5. However, there was a bimodal distribution of scores with a cluster that was close to the lower end of the middle 50 percent range, and one unusually low score of 29, which can easily pull down the mean of such a small sample. This single score was also the only one below the lower 25 percent cutoff point of 35. At the other end were seven individuals with scores in the top 25 percent range, which was defined by a cutoff score of 45. The range and distribution of these scores merited particular attention in evaluating the group. Also, it could be especially important to find out the basis of the very low score of the one individual.

The mean for total commitment in the group was 130.2, considerably higher than the 121.7 of the normative sample. Seven members were in the top 25 percent and two were in the bottom 25 percent. An executive looking at the overall pattern for this group might conclude that, with a few exceptions (several scores below the 25 percent cutoff), the picture was a good one. Although commitment to work was higher than in the other two categories, all three areas were acceptable because they were above the normative mean. This would certainly be a reasonable conclusion, but unfortunately it overlooks the potential for examining the inner workings of the group to see what similarities and differences determined the commitment scores. Furthermore, what the executive might see is a mirror image held at a distance, one that fails to reveal the sharp features and blemishes that only a close look can provide.

Before we begin the closer examination, there is one additional set of statistics that proved to be most interesting. In the larger normative samples the correlations among the three dimensions of commitment all were significant. (These figures are reported in Chapter 4.) For the bank group this turned out not to be the case. While work commitment and organizational commitment correlated at the same level (r = 0.55) as in the larger sample, there was no relationship between co-worker commitment and either of the other dimensions (r = −0.06 for work and r = 0.16 for organization). It will prove to be particularly important to review the item scores in this regard.

Item-by-item analysis. In examining the data item by item, some judgment had to be exercised about what could be considered high scores as opposed to low ones. Although it may be somewhat arbitrary, it was decided, after looking at the distribution of the thirty-item scores, to use 4.0 as the lower cutoff point and 5.0 as the upper cutoff point to determine low and high item scores, respectively. Thirteen of the items fell within the middle grouping, nine fell below 4.0, and eight fell above 5.0.

Looking at the work identification items with the highest scores (above 5.0), it may be said that this group of employees enjoyed its work, took pride in the quality of its work, did not feel that its workday dragged and seemed endless, and constantly strove to improve skills. The only item that clearly scored relatively low (below 4.0) pertained to becoming so absorbed in work that everything else got shut out. This low score may, in fact, have been a positive sign relative to a team effort, since teamwork usually requires attention to the work of others.

With respect to co-worker identification, two items scored very high, one related to readiness to help co-workers and the other showing personal satisfaction from working with others. There were four items with low scores. These indicated an overall tendency of group members to mind their own business, to not mix work and friendship, to make sure they finished their own work before checking to see if others needed help, and to not view losing department members as a family loss. These findings proved to be especially important to the team-building effort, since two of the items became a focal point for change.

Organizational identification showed two high-scoring items, one indicating pleasure from the organization's achievements and the other reflecting attention to information about how the organization was doing. These two items were related to one another. The low-scoring items indicated that the group did not tend to become defensive about negative comments about the organization, usually was not ready to let another department's needs take priority over its own, even for the sake of the organization, and did not believe that the world would be a better place if more organizations were like theirs. The one item in this category that proved to be especially important was the one related to interdepartmental priorities. One of the problems observed at the bank for some time was counterproductive conflicts across department lines, in many cases resulting in some damage to customer service. Its importance was reinforced by the findings related to co-worker commitment. Two of the items in that category reflected a need for the group to better understand the importance of member interdependence with respect to tasks.

As the consultant to the group, I decided to focus attention on the issue of task interdependence. It seemed clear that the level of commitment of the members of the department was, overall, quite strong in all three areas. This provided a solid base to build on. The individuals seemed to be at least minimally aware of how others were doing and ready to help them out, but there was a tendency toward territoriality. One of the paradoxes inherent in a team effort is the importance of people minding each others' business. This runs counter to traditional western values that encourage one to mind one's *own* business and counter to traditional management practices that require employees to get their own work finished before attending to anything else.

To bring the issue to the group's attention, I decided to create a situation that would illustrate work interdependence. Some readers may be familiar with the classic "Broken Squares Exercise." For the sake of those who are not, let me provide a capsule description.

The "Broken Squares Exercise" essentially involves a group of five individuals required to assemble five squares from fifteen pieces distributed among the members of the group. The task is finished when there is a completed square in front of each person. All pieces must be used, no talking is allowed, no individual may help another, no pieces may be taken from anyone else, and pieces may only be passed to another person. Because there are a number of obstacles to achieving the objective, as well as the obvious constraints on communication, each group member must pay particular attention to what is happening with the others, as well as to the process as a whole. The exercise almost invariably illustrates the nature of task interdependence more clearly than intellectual discussion alone. The discussion is important, but it is powerfully reinforced by the group's experience.

It was possible to divide the twenty members of the department into four groups of five, which generated four different group patterns and an atmosphere of competition, which provided the basis for a later discussion of interdependence among departments in the bank. The learning outcome of the exercise proved powerful enough for the group to review some of its formal procedures and informal norms, with an eye toward continuous monitoring of task interdependence. The most difficult change required of the group had to do with the basic belief that people should mind their own business. The members literally asked each other for the right to violate that long-cherished belief.

The group then began to explore other aspects of the data, with special attention to the commitment scores in the organizational category. The bimodal distribution of scores turned out to be directly related to tenure. The three lowest scores came from relatively new hires (including the score of 29, which came from the newest member of the department), while the high scores came from a large cluster of people who had been with the bank for many years. This finding, while admittedly based on a single case example, did confirm the importance of measuring organizational commitment independently of the other areas. In fact, the employee with the 29 scored well within the group norm in the other two categories, especially in identification with co-workers. This last point is consistent with the group's willingness to help each other and the very high scores on the item related to bringing new people on board.

The discussion of the correlations among the three measures of commitment proved to be very enlightening, especially since I was able to compare the bank group's results with the results from the large samples. When I showed them that members of the group who identified most strongly with their work were also those who identified most strongly with the bank as an organization, and vice versa, no one seemed at all surprised. They agreed, in effect, that their commitment to the work depended directly on the degree to which the bank let them manage their own work and encouraged their involvement in how the bank operated. In other words, they were saying that the bank's management practices, as well as its reward system, directly affected their commitment to their work. They also felt that the absence of any correlation between co-worker commitment and either of the other two categories made sense, given the lack of agreed-upon requirements for job interdependence. The conclusion they drew was that the next step was to focus on the basics of teamwork.

The Management Team. The group was composed of the twelve officers and division managers of a company. It was an all white male group, represented all the major functional areas of the company, all but one were college graduates, and five had advanced degrees. Also, all but one had been with the company for more than ten years; the one exception was a recently hired vice president for research and development.

What precipitated the need for a team development effort was the suggestion of the new man who, entering with an outside perspective, quickly became aware of the amount of time wasted in planning meetings and the highly individualized orientations of his colleagues. It was more like the pooled interdependence of a baseball team than the reciprocal interdependence of a basketball team. He had been through some sessions on team building at his previous place of employment, had found them useful, although his own background in research had not really prepared him to work collaboratively, and suggested that the group he had just joined might find such an approach useful. Initially the group resisted and put the idea on the back burner.

A few months later one of the other members shared his frustration with the lack of effective cooperation within the team. Decisions seemed to be made without complete follow-through and implementation.

My entry as a consultant to the group came as a result of my acquaintance with one of its members. He knew that team development was one of my areas of expertise, and he felt that I would be a good fit for the group. When I shared with him my research interests and how I would like to use the CDI as part of the data gathering, he became quite enthusiastic because he was sure that a group of engineering and technical people would be comfortable with quantitative data as a foundation for team building.

It struck me at the time that the kinds of personalities typical of this type of organization are not naturally attuned to the interpersonal issues of a team effort. Therefore, the use of numbers, comparisons, and profiles just might provide the comfort zone needed to guarantee participation. This effort might have worked using a less formal approach, but I was convinced that the quantitative approach was appropriate for this group. After an introductory meeting of several hours, the group members filled out the CDI for me to score and organize for feedback during a two-day retreat.

The CDI data proved to be interesting and useful, but it also posed the danger of becoming a sidetrack of the most important issues. Those members of the group interested in the quantitative material wanted to spend hours just playing with the data to see what they could extract. I had to help them maintain their focus on the issues at hand and to use the data as a source of information about those issues.

The CDI means for total scores and subscores were all in the top 25 percent for managers. The means for commitment to work and to the organization were both exceptionally high scores of 50, while the mean for the co-worker category was on the borderline of the 75th percentile, a score of 46. These results were consistent with my expectations and similar to the profile of the bank group. What is even more interesting is that the key items that helped target the issues for this group to deal with were exactly the same as those identified in the bank group. The implications of this finding will be discussed in some detail later.

There was one member of the group whose scores in all categories fell into the middle 50 percent range and whose co-worker commitment score (36) was at the very bottom of that range. This result alone led to some intense discussion about that person's disillusionment with the company in recent years, his increasing feelings of isolation from his colleagues, and his desire to find more challenges. He still liked the work that he did (his commitment to work score was at the 75th percentile), but that was not enough to keep him motivated. Although the group made some effort to bring him into a more central and active role related to future planning, which he did appreciate, he did leave the company some months later to start a small business of his own, a dream he had for many years.

The item-by-item analysis used the same cutoff points used in the bank example. Mean scores above 5.0 were considered strong areas and mean scores below 4.0 were considered weak areas. The items that reflected the strengths of the group in the work category included enjoyment of work, pride in quality of work, not watching the clock, day not dragging, and ability to concentrate on work. The strengths in the co-worker area included readiness to help co-workers, valuing interactions, and helping new members come aboard. In the organization category the strong items included pleasure in the organization's achievements, paying attention to information about the organization, having a sense of where one's own work fit into the overall system, and thinking about a project even after it moved to another department.

With respect to the weak areas, in the work category the only item that scored below 4.0 pertained to the work being its own reward. In the co-worker category the low items related to minding one's own business, mixing work and friendship, completing one's own work before paying attention to others' work, and feeling that co-workers are like family. Finally, in the organizational category the only item that scored low related to letting the priorities of another department take precedence over one's own department for the sake of the organization.

As in the bank group there was a strong foundation for team building, given the number of items and the kinds of items that reflected the commitment strengths of the group. The focus for discussion and work was on the issues indicated by the low scoring items, in particular those in the co-worker category, where most of the low scores occurred. Again, as in the bank group, the lack of cooperation both among the team members and among the departments or groups they represented turned out to be at the heart of many difficulties the group had been experiencing.

Having grown up in technical fields where the focus of one's attention had always been on doing one's own work and where the reward system reinforced that behavior, the team members had never really paid adequate attention to the larger context of their actions and, in particular, just how these actions might affect the operations of the other members of the team. While they liked and respected each other, and while each was ready to help when called upon, what was missing was the ongoing attention to each other's needs and the willingness to let those needs take priority over one's own.

Most of the two-day retreat was devoted to cooperation issues. Using the definition of teamwork as a guide, the group examined the norms and ground rules that needed to be changed in order to facilitate and maintain interdependence within the team and among the groups each member represented. Some renegotiations had to occur, so the time was structured to allow whatever combinations of people were necessary to accomplish them.

Some reflections. In thinking back on these two cases the similarities in the patterns of results struck me as more than coincidental. I believe it is a reflection of the kind of basic individualistic orientation with which most of us, expecially men, have grown up, plus the reinforcement received when we are educated with a focus on individual performance and narrowly specialized professions. It is a wonder that we can ever build effective teamwork in organizations; it requires putting aside a great many of the assumptions and habits that have led to success in the past.

Weisbord places interdependence at the top of his list of conditions for successful team building (1987, p. 299). Evidently, our ability to establish interdependent working relationships does not come easily and may even be an uphill effort in many cases. Today's organizations talk a great deal about the importance of a team effort, but few seem to really understand the extent to which that very concept goes against the grain of so much of past orientation toward work and models of leadership (see Bradford and Cohen, 1984, on heroic leadership). The faith that people can work effectively in teams as long as they can maintain group cohesiveness and member bonding is not enough. The sociotechnical experts found the key many years ago: Understand the nature of the technical system's requirements, which include task interdependence, before designing the social system that best meets those requirements. That kind of thinking was missing in both the bank group and the management team described here. I did not carry out a sociotechnical analysis in either case, but the connections between the technical and social aspects of the groups became the leverage points for improvement.

Informal Methods: Commitment Indicators

Many organizational development consultants may prefer to use methods of data gathering and diagnosis more informal than the CDI requires. Since the measurement methods were based upon the reported observations of practicing managers, it seems quite appropriate to use one's own observations of employees' behavior and expressed attitudes as useful indicators of commitment in each of the three areas. As discussed in Chapter 4, the thirty phrases that formed the basis of the CDI can be used informally as *commitment indicators*—a way to take a reading on employees' behavior and attitudes. Some of the phrases clearly relate to observable behavior, others require some careful attention to consistent patterns, and others may necessitate direct inquiries into employees' beliefs.

One of the skills of an effective manager is to be able to gather useful information simply by walking around. As described by Peters and Waterman (1982), it is possible to develop a fairly accurate picture of employee commitment through simple, unobtrusive observation. This is probably a good place to begin, provided that one has in mind some guidelines for observation. The commitment indicators can provide them. It is important to keep in mind that no one or two indicators necessarily reflect commitment, since any given behavior or attitude can have multiple causes. It is the overall constellation of items that defines commitment. Furthermore, it is not necessary to use only those indicators related to the CDI in making observations. The thirty phrases can be much too limiting.

What is important is to pay attention to the kinds of behavior and attitudes one would expect to reflect each category of commitment. In the general descriptions that follow, the italicized phrases relate directly to the CDI items; other phrases (not italicized) fall into the same categories and may be used as additional indicators of a given area of commitment. Anyone using this informal approach may wish to develop additional indicators appropriate for a particular situation, as long as they are consistent with the theoretical framework. Let us look at each category of commitment.

Identification with Work. As one goes about one's daily work activities as a manager one probably is aware of those employees who tend to become *highly absorbed in their work,* almost to the point where they do not even know that a manager or anyone else, for that matter, is around. These people seem to have extraordinary powers of *concentration, shutting out any distraction.* One may notice that they are *not clock-watchers,* and they often report that they wish they had more time to get the work done. Evidently, for these employees *the work does not drag and seem endless.* Nonverbal cues, such as smiling or laughing from time to time, would suggest *great enjoyment of the work* and probably that *the work tends to be its own reward.* Furthermore, these usually are the same people who demonstrate obvious *pride in the quality of their work* and never cease to *strive to improve their skills.* Finally, short of being workaholics, these employees *obtain considerable need satisfaction from their jobs, often thinking about work when not at work.* They talk a great deal about their jobs outside of the work setting, and they often use their evening and weekend time to "catch up on things."

Any good manager would be pleased to have employees who behave that way, but many tend to kill the goose that laid the golden egg by trying to make sure that the behavior continues. They take behavior and attitudes that have emerged from within the workers and establish formal procedures to document them. Genuine commitment gets translated into "long working hours," then into "working at least 55 hours a week," and eventually into "coming in at 7 a.m. and leaving at 7 p.m." This phenomenon is described by Steele and Jenks (1977) in their discussion of organizational norms. They point out the ways in which emergent norms that enhance employee performance can get replaced by formal requirements that often diminish performance. This pattern illustrates how easily a manager can take employee behavior based on commitment and move it to behavior based on compliance. The behavior itself may look the same, but the former situation is self-sustaining, while the latter tends to be dependent upon the presence of managerial control.

Identification with Co-Workers. Although there are varying degrees to which people are interpersonally or socially oriented, the nature of work today requires attention to task interdependence. At a minimum, employees need to appreciate the ways in which their own work efforts affect and are affected by the efforts of their co-workers. Over time, even the most introverted individuals begin to develop a genuine appreciation and caring for their colleagues. They not only become *aware of how they are doing,* but are *ready to offer help when necessary,* sometimes to the point of putting aside their own work and *letting a co-worker's needs come first.* It seems important to them *not to mind their own business;* they are each others' business. And it does not take an acute mind to notice behavior patterns that reflect these attitudes. Employees tend to seek each other out on a social basis, indicating that *they are willing to mix work and friendship.* Their greetings to one another when arriving at work show that *they really look forward to seeing each other.* One can feel *a sense of family on the job,* but not one that shuts out new members. In fact, along with *efforts to stay connected with each other,* co-workers extend a *welcome to new members.* In general, it is apparent that the *relationships* among the members of the group *provide them with strong need satisfaction.*

One of the issues with which groups struggle is the balance between group needs and individual needs. Conformity pressures that stifle individuality tend to reduce an individual's commitment to co-workers, but might not be obvious. Conformity pressure results in compliance to group norms and not identification with the group.

Many so-called teams have been known to fall apart under stress because of a lack of adequate individual commitment to the team when times are tough. Such a group suffers from what is often described as "groupthink." Unfortunately, this phenomenon is difficult to distinguish from genuine group commitment under normal conditions because the overt behavior and expressed attitudes are the same.

One of the signs that genuine commitment may be lacking is members of a group complaining about poor decisions after they leave a meeting and not while they are in it. Even the most successful teams are prone to a sense of invulnerability, which can lead to discouraging dissenting opinion, so it may be especially important for a manager striving to maximize commitment to be acutely aware of this danger at a time when there may be little willingness to break the team's bubble of success. By way of contrast, a team that is in crisis (feels like a defeated group), can also close ranks and put pressure on members to conform to behavior and attitudes that block genuine self-analysis. Again, compliance to the shared delusion can be mistaken for commitment to a truly shared belief.

Identification with the Organization. Commitment to the organization might be more difficult to assess than the other two kinds of commitment; it might require a more direct inquiry on the part of a manager into what the employees are thinking or feeling. However, just listening to informal conversations and watching for reactions to critical events can reveal a great deal about peoples' identification with the organization. Two contrasting examples might help to illustrate this point.

I had an opportunity to talk with several engineers from a high tech manufacturer that was struggling to get itself out of the loss column. It was using a combination of furloughs and layoffs to deal with the short-run financial problem, without giving much consideration to the long-term effects. The engineers told me that people were walking around depressed and angry about the way top management was handling the problem. Little effort was being given to informing, much less involving, employees in what was happening. Many stated that their once strong belief in the company had dwindled to disillusionment, and they no longer cared whether management turned things around. This attitude could be seen on the faces of many employees and not just in their behavior and expressed attitudes. The engineers told me that most employees still cared about their work and continued to work well as team members on projects, but overall cooperation among departments had deteriorated. Responsiveness to company-wide pronouncements or directives, especially from the top, were viewed cynically and responded to only half-heartedly.

I witnessed a very different scenario at another company that was struggling with similar financial difficulties. Management made every effort to keep people informed, even when the news was very bad. Those who had to be laid off were given strong encouragement and, where possible, helped to find other jobs. It was important to the company to treat those who were leaving with as much care and respect as possible. Those who remained in their jobs expressed real pride in their company's philosophy and, despite wage freezes, continued to put forth maximum effort on behalf of the organization. There were constant conversations over coffee, in the cafeteria, and on the shop floor about company problems and how important it was for productivity to be maintained. I was really surprised to see the level of energy throughout the company, given all the uncertainty it faced. People were sad about losing some members of their work teams, but they seemed to rise above those feelings. As one worker said to me, "The boss is being straight with us, this plant has a reputation for good work, so I'll do my part to keep it going."

It is easy to see how important it is, if one wants to foster a high level of commitment to the organization, to keep employees *informed as to how the organization is doing.* Since the principal responsibility for this rests with top management, the *behavior of the CEO can have a major impact on employees' feelings.* The two examples showed sharp contrasts in the way employees saw their roles relative to the company goals. In the first case, employees seemed to have lost all sense of *congruence between their individual goals and the goals of the organization.* This was not true in the second case, where employees had a strong sense of that congruence, as well as a clear picture of *how their individual efforts contributed to the total effort.* In addition, it was evident that the second group of employees was feeling the pain of the company's problem and would, by implication, *take pleasure in its successes,* certainly for personal or self-serving reasons, but also from a sense of pride in the company.

It was interesting to note, however, that many of the supervisors and managers I talked to at the second company were both openly critical of their own company and, from what many reported to me, *ready to defend the company when outsiders criticized it.* This clearly was not true of the first example. While many employees seemed to like their work and valued their co-workers, they also were more than ready to take jobs elsewhere; they *saw greener pastures in other companies.* Gone were the days when they were *seeing their organization in an ideal light.* The one attitude that both companies had in common was a tendency to maintain strong departmental identities. Neither paid *attention to the work flow beyond departmental lines,* much less *allowed organizational priorities to take precedence over departmental ones.* It happens that in the second example the company had identified interdepartmental relations as the next issue for a major educational effort.

Conclusions

There are definite advantages and disadvantages to the formal and informal approaches to diagnosing organizational problems. While the formal methods are systematic and give one a greater sense of confidence in the picture that emerges, they also can create strong resistance from employees, especially in organizations where surveys tend to become a way of life. Furthermore, such methods often feel like an invasion of privacy to those "asked" to fill them out. The more informal approaches, on the other hand, seem less threatening and, in an organization that is striving to become more participative, more consistent with the espoused philosophy.

To the extent that management thinks in action-research terms, an organization probably will find that it can use a mixture of the formal and informal, since the data in either case is fed back to the employees themselves for development purposes. In fact, I have found that employee-initiated data gathering tends to use very formal and carefully planned procedures. My own experience suggests that as long as employees feel in control of the process, the threat often associated with company-wide surveys is reduced considerably.

It also is useful to use informal observations to corroborate formal data, or vice versa. However, in those instances where the two do not seem to say the same thing, it is important to avoid dismissing one or the other set of data out of hand. Each could reflect a valid picture, and the apparent discrepancy can be important information.

Chapter 8 discusses the different profiles (combinations of high and low scores) that the three category scores generate. The profiles provide a diagnostic framework for understanding individuals and groups in an organization as well as the organization as a whole.

Chapter 8

Commitment Profiles

The commitment profiles presented in this chapter admittedly are extremes in the sense that they are generated from combinations of hypothetically very high and very low scores on the three dimensions of commitment, as reflected in either CDI scores or from observations using commitment indicators. Since the scores actually exist on a continuum for each dimension, it would be possible to generate an infinite number of profiles. Therefore, in considering each of the eight described here, think in terms of this proposition: "To the extent to which this combination is true, the following picture is likely to occur."

Although in most cases an organization will see as desirable high levels in all three areas, that may not be a valid or practical assumption to make. There are jobs that might be best performed by someone with a profile that is different from the so-called ideal. Therefore, we will examine not only the problems that ensue from profiles different from the ideal, but offer some suggestions as to when they may be highly desirable.

This chapter is divided into three sections: a discussion of each of the eight commitment profiles and how they originally were developed; case examples of each profile; and a discussion of the circumstances under which some of the profiles might be more desirable or suited to organizational objectives than others.

Development of the Commitment Profiles

The method used to generate the profiles was similar to that used to create the list of commitment indicators and, subsequently, the CDI. The same groups of managers attending executive education sessions at the University of New Hampshire were used to generate the profiles from a practicing manager's perspective. In addition, however, colleagues of mine were consulted. Combining their experiences with mine, the profiles were refined and more clearly defined. The eight profiles are not intended to be all-inclusive, but only illustrative of the kinds of behavior and attitudes one would expect to find given the particular level of commitment in each category. Each of the profiles is depicted graphically. Included is a table that summarizes the profiles, their principal characteristics, some typical problems associated with each, and ways to deal with those problems.

The Profiles

System Performers

In a high performing system, the principal focus of all employees is on maximizing production and maintaining high quality. Such an organization depends upon the presence of what I call *system performers:* employees with high levels of commitment in all three categories. In discussing the impact of sociotechnical design, Cal Pava describes a high performing system: "Workers are oriented to produce collaboratively a tangible product, instead of being assigned to an isolated, repetitive operation with no apparent connection to an overall result. Also, work group members are encouraged to become increasingly skilled at managing their own operation. Finally, financial rewards are greater for members who learn more to help the group manage itself" (1983, p. 31). Pava also stresses the importance of long-range thinking and coordination among work groups.

In essence, a high performing system, whether it is a small or large organization, is one that operates at peak effectiveness and efficiency and maximizes both the quantity and quality of its product or service, with a minimum of delays or turn-around time from start to finish. Such a system requires the highest levels of employee commitment in all three categories, especially where reciprocal interdependence is great. Energy is high and members share a common sense of purpose and pride in the organization as a whole, as well as in their own work unit (see Figure 8.1).

The high level of employee commitment in all three categories, which reflects the presence of system performers, does not guarantee a high performing system. For that to occur it is also necessary to have the financial, material, and technological resources that enable system performers to produce at a high level. We are all too familiar with organizations that lack those resources and, despite having the best people working for them, go under. Also, we have seen the effects of economic factors that do not discriminate between the companies with the best and those with the worst management practices.

Let us look at some examples of system performers.

The Computer Manufacturer. I had an opportunity to visit the Enfield, Connecticut, plant of Digital Equipment Corporation (DEC) a number of years ago, around the time it was first developing its sociotechnical approach to

Figure 8.1. System Performers

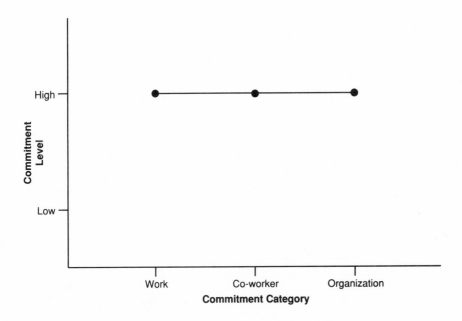

manufacturing. This particular unit was experimenting with a zero-inventory, high-performance system, with roughly 120 people responsible for assembling modules for a mainframe computer. By involving all employees in planning and development, educating them in every phase and aspect of the work, and designing the work environment in a way that kept all workers aware of the total system in operation at all times, a sense of being a team emerged that resulted in production surpassing all expectations in both quantity and quality.

Very little external supervision or control was needed to keep people working at their maximums. Whenever there were absences or someone needed help, someone else was ready to jump in and put forth the extra effort to keep the system going. I observed that employees seemed to be having fun with their jobs (even routine ones) because they felt themselves to be part of something exciting. One woman was working at what seemed to me to be an incredible pace, yet she told me that she was determined to "beat my number from yesterday—and do the same tomorrow."

The atmosphere was that of a sports team having a winning season. It was energetic and spirited; it definitely was driven by unusually high levels of employee commitment. The members identified with the goals of the system, with each other as part of a team, and with the particular tasks they were performing. In an article in the *National Productivity Review* (1986), Barcy

Proctor, human resources manager and a member of the original design team for the facility, described the culture as "one in which there is a strong emphasis on working together, teaching each other, and on sharing in general. The level of responsibility placed upon people here is exceptionally high" (p. 263).

One important difference between this setting and many others that emphasize team performance is that the DEC operation also placed great emphasis on total system awareness, keeping employees identified not just with their own teams but also with the whole plant. I chose this as an example of system performers, but I also consider it an example of a high performing system.

Other Examples. Some of the organizations identified as excellent by Peters and Waterman (1982) seem to be characterized by high levels of commitment to work, people, and organization. It is evident from some of the authors' descriptive data that identification with organizational mission is a strong factor; just how strong the levels of commitment are to specific tasks and to people is difficult to say. A study of each company in some depth would be necessary to find out. I would predict, however, that these companies, if they are to remain excellent, would have to foster all three kinds of identification on a long-term basis—if they are not already doing so.

Although a number of major corporations recently have been cited as examples of excellence including General Electric, IBM, Hewlett Packard, and others, one of the truly outstanding organizations in recent years has been Corning, Inc. The very fact that Corning was written up glowingly in *Business Week* twice in a six-month period is testimony to its outstanding achievements as a well-managed company.

The articles (December 17, 1990 and May 13, 1991) about Corning clearly reflected management practices that foster the development of system performers. Employees at all levels were given a great deal of responsibility; the work generally was carried out in teams, with members imposing their own controls and discipline, if needed; workers described themselves as multiskilled and dedicated to product quality, constant improvement, and customer service. The company was committed to upgrading the educational levels of employees; layers of management had been eliminated in order to empower employees to manage themselves; and an assertive effort to increase gender, racial, and cultural diversity had been instituted, with already measurable success.

Team Performers

High performing teams are on the increase in modern organizations. The success of such teams depends upon the presence of what are referred to here as *team performers*. Bradford and Cohen (1984) emphasize the importance of developing high performing teams as a way to achieve excellence: "Such

Figure 8.2. Team Performers

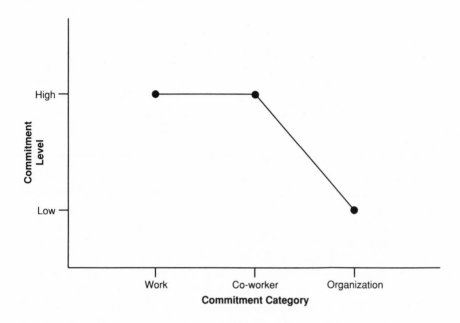

a group produces high-quality solutions, provides coordination among members, and is the vehicle for shared responsibility in managing the department'' (p. 170).

The norms of high performing teams tend to be very strong and congruent with the goals of the group. However, there is also a tendency to create strong group boundaries that can impede cooperation with other groups in the system. In contrast to the high performing system, in which groups maintain organization-wide commitment, the high performing team can exist in relative isolation and out of touch with its effect on other parts of the system. Interdependence is recognized and honored within the team, but not to the same degree in relation to other teams (see Figure 8.2). How serious the consequences are depends on the nature of the organization and the particular role a given team plays in that organization.

As in the case of a high performing system, whether team performers actually can become a high performing team is not just a matter of high commitment to the work and to co-workers; it also depends upon the availability of resources to do the work, especially the latest technology, and on the economic environment that demands the products and/or services that the organization provides. Sometimes a terrific team of employees has no market or demand for its work and can be eliminated for that reason.

The Research and Development Group. This profile is common in organizations today, especially where highly skilled young people work together at tasks that require frequent interactions and result in strong bonding. The boundaries are established quickly and firmly, and the performance levels of the group members, as well as the total team, tend to be very high. One research and development (R&D) department I visited even engaged in daily outside recreation, and the members seemed to be virtually inseparable. Asked about other parts of the company, they knew very little and seemed to care less. What little they did know tended to be negative and produced derogatory comments. "Those guys in sales look good only because of our success. We keep the company two jumps ahead of the competition; that's what sells the product." This was a typical remark. Although this R&D group did identify to some extent with the company as a whole, most members indicated a much stronger sense of being part of a team that could function successfully anywhere.

Is this something to be concerned about? One might argue that having high commitment in two out of three areas is not so bad and may be enough to guarantee long-term success anyway. If there is little or no interdependence between R&D and other departments or groups, no action is required. If, however, information flow among the departments begins to suffer or people start to waste time in competitive bickering, some attention must be given to the issue of low identification with the organization as a whole. Or, if the isolation of an R&D group results in a loss of adequate contact with top management, the danger of stereotyping increases. Top management can be perceived as "doing very little anyway," and the R&D unit can be perceived by top management as "a bunch of mavericks who want to run their own show."

Efforts to correct or prevent dysfunctional problems of this kind must not be arbitrary if they are to be effective; they should grow out of the overall, long-range plans of the company. Where problems and conflicts already have occurred, it is useful to create cross-group task forces to diagnose and solve them. But most useful are actions that foster total company identification before problems occur. By drawing upon the resources, ideas, and aspirations of people from a variety of groups and levels in the organization in ways that produce interaction and, ultimately, the integration of those ideas, it is possible to enhance company identification.

Contributing Performers

Most of the high performing, highly committed employees in Company A could be called *contributing performers.* In fact, I would surmise that the vast majority of the best employees in today's organizations fall into this category. This is not to say that they are not good team players relative to their co-workers, but as in the bank case, their reward systems tend to build

Figure 8.3. Contributing Performers

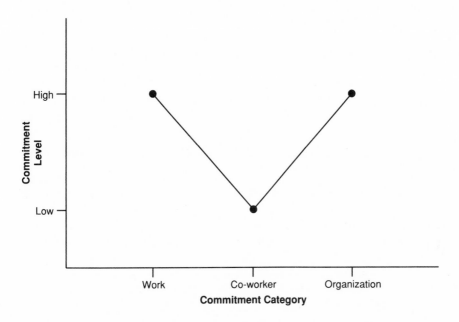

the strongest levels of commitment to work and to the organization. And as long as the company can profit from this situation (see Figure 8.3), it will see little reason to change it. As Robert Keidel describes it, it is akin to the mentality of a baseball team (1985).

Highly skilled technical personnel often fit this profile well, as do really good sales people who are not out to serve just their own needs. In a discussion with a vice president for sales at a large company, the significance of this profile as compared to the next one (individualistic performers) provided some valuable insight into the difference between sales people who leave almost before the company has fully trained them and those who stay for the long run. That difference seems to lie in the level of identification with the organization and not just the job. The implications for hiring can be extremely important. A company must decide what it needs and then select on that basis; the contributing performer may be desirable for one situation but the individualistic performer (see next section) may be just fine for another. To develop the former, it is obvious that special efforts need to be made to build organizational identification; this is not an issue for the individualistic performer.

Let us look at two examples.

The Psychology Department. A psychology department of eighteen members at a medium-sized midwestern university suffered for years from internal conflicts that were damaging the quality of education and the reputation of the department. The students were tense and often felt like scapegoats for the faculty members' conflicts. It was evident from their individual reputations and scholarship that the faculty was highly prestigious. Also, because the university was considered to be excellent, most members of the department felt a strong identification with it. Consequently, the faculty members tended to remain in the department and carry out their teaching and research individually, but rarely met to create a coherent and forward-looking curriculum. Each course was fine, but the program was not well developed. Little collegiality emerged, except in a few cases of untenured younger members who sought support and protection for their careers by banding together as a subgroup of the faculty.

The chair of the department was an industrial psychologist and a member of the Academy of Management. In a conversation with a colleague from another university the chair began to unload her feelings of frustration with her department. The colleague suggested she hire an outside consultant to do some team development work, much as such efforts are conducted in industry and business.

When she suggested this idea to the faculty at the next meeting, it was rejected very quickly with, "We're psychologists, why should we hire another psychologist to tell us what to do about our problems? Besides, it would be a little humiliating, to say the least."

Things got worse, until one day individual members of the faculty came to the chair and stated privately that they thought the consultant idea was a good one. It became clear that a group norm in faculty meetings was, "Never admit your problems openly," which had masked each member's true attitude.

To make a long story short, a consultant was hired, he established a relationship with the group that fostered more open and direct confrontation of problems, and ultimately helped the group develop an overarching goal for the department while supporting the individual efforts of each faculty member. Many of the fears about losing one's individuality for the sake of the group disappeared, and new norms (in the form of explicit ground rules) emerged that created a healthy educational climate for both faculty and students. Although some of the old tensions among faculty members seemed to hang on, they no longer were played out in classroom behavior and student-faculty relationships.

As the interactions among the faculty members increased, they began to really appreciate each other as talented individuals and to develop a strong sense of identification as a social system. This became evident when someone outside the department criticized a department member to a colleague from within the department. The outsider was promptly criticized and told that his judgment was based on bad information and that he really did not know the person well enough to criticize him. This reaction came from someone who frequently was at odds with that same person in faculty meetings.

What used to be everybody's business had become family business; what an individual could say freely to a member of the family could not be said by anyone outside the family. This was a clear indication that cohesiveness had developed where it had been missing. Now commitment was high in all three areas.

Direct Sales Companies. Successful direct sales organizations, like Amway, Mary Kay, Shaklee, Discovery Toys, and others, depend upon a high level of employee commitment to both the job (selling the product) and to the organization. In her book *Charismatic Capitalism* (1989), Nicole Biggart shows how direct sales organizations build commitment from the employees' powerful identification with a highly charismatic leader and with the mission of the organization. Biggart's research indicates that "maintaining social order and soliciting commitment in direct selling organizations, because of their charismatic character, is very different from the bureaucratic controls used by firms" (p. 134). She goes on to point out that while business firms usually have the legal authority to control employees, direct sales organizations have no legal control over employees and, therefore, must exercise control socially and ideologically.

In essence, successful direct sales organizations can be described as made up of contributing performers. In some respects, however, it could be argued that there also is a strong team identification in many of these organizations, especially in those, like Mary Kay, that hold frequent meetings and generate a kind of team spirit. However, the day-to-day work is not carried out in a way that requires attention to cooperation among employees. It could be described as a form of pooled interdependence, which benefits from the social bonding and shared mission of the employees. But this is the only sense in which I would classify such an organization as composed of system performers.

Individualistic Performers

Temporary employees fit the *individualistic performer* profile nicely. The employer wants a high level of performance for a defined time period and does not plan to orient the person to the organization or be concerned about membership issues. Compliance to the task requirements may even be adequate for the employer, but if a minimum of supervision is desirable, it would be best to have someone who does identify strongly with the work itself (see Figure 8.4).

Where many organizations make their mistake is in hiring people who fit the individualistic performer profile for jobs that really demand a more long-term commitment to the organization and/or to the department. Then, when the employees transfer to jobs that serve their needs more, the employer

Figure 8.4. Individualistic Performers

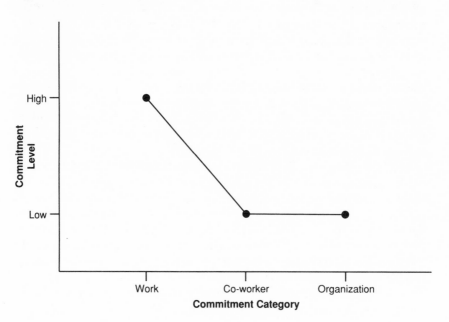

is surprised and disappointed. Part of the problem is in the selection process and part is in the ongoing management practices that do or do not foster commitment to co-workers or the organization.

If what is needed is a temporary sales force, the individualistic performer is the right profile; but if what is needed is a salesperson who also markets the company, the contributing performer is a better choice. As will be seen in the next example, some professions or occupations prepare people to do their thing, do it well, and not pay a lot of attention to what others need. Then, when they go to work in a setting that requires high task interdependence, things do not work out in the best interests of the system (group or organization).

The Magazine. This scenario occurred at a weekly magazine. Success of the enterprise depended upon the effective flow of operations from writers to editors to designers to production and, finally, to sales. Snags at any point disrupted the total system; therefore, everyone needed to be aware of and committed to the total process and to the effect on others of one's own actions (or inactions).

Unfortunately, the writers too often tended to be committed primarily to the quality of their own efforts, frequently came in late with stories, and were hard to find when needed for changes in stories. The result was constant tension and uncertainty as deadlines came and went and production people anticipated rushed jobs and late working hours. Direct appeals to writers and editors fell on deaf ears.

As is the case in many publishing houses, newspapers, magazines, and the like, writers and editors often are perceived to have (and may indeed actually have) the highest status of any of the professional groups (e.g., designers, production people, or sales people). Consequently, a sense of elitism (with all the special privileges) develops that works against the level of cooperation necessary to get the work done most effectively. The common purpose—usually a high quality product—gets subverted in favor of more personal ends (e.g., a noted byline).

I am not suggesting that writers or editors are inherently self-serving people; many may be, as in every profession. What I am suggesting is that the behavior described is to a great extent attributable to the situation and the culture. The sales of a publication—and the reactions of the public—usually have an obvious relationship to the content of the material. Design and format tend to affect these outcomes in more subtle ways. Furthermore, as noted earlier, the larger the operation, the more likely it is that people's interactions will be *within* professional boundaries instead of *across* those boundaries. This fosters even more obstacles to cooperation.

The writer's strong identification as a writer is vital to the organization. The issue to be managed is that of extending that identification across professional boundaries and to connect it to some overall, long-range vision shared by all. Planning meetings (usually for a given issue) need to include people from all groups. Although the actual production process or the imposition of advertising comes late in the sequence of events, including those functions early in the planning process can serve a number of purposes:

1. It enables those whose work occurs later in the sequence to anticipate what is coming down the line and to raise any potential problems early enough to have them handled in advance.
2. It enables those whose work occurs early in the sequence to see how their efforts affect others, especially when it comes to scheduling and deadlines.
3. It builds a sense of common purpose.
4. It places all groups on an equal footing when needed.
5. It fosters an open sharing of vital information.

The net result is commitment to the broadest possible goals and to all others who share those goals. It seems easy enough to accomplish, but it seems to occur too rarely. It may be easier for people to stay focused on their own work, especially when they feel overloaded, than to put forth the extra effort on behalf of others and the total organization.

Team Players

Employees who have spent many years in the same organization may become strongly attached to their departments and to the organization overall without really growing in their own jobs. It is as though they are on automatic pilot; they continue to do all the routine tasks well, but no longer with any real sense of involvement. They are the *team players*. What keeps them going is the support of their co-workers and a belief in what the organization stands for. Team players (see Figure 8.5) often are excellent candidates for burnout, because they have long since lost the joy of the work that they do.

A good example occurs in the health professions, where individuals feel very strongly about the value of medical care, would never think of letting down colleagues with whom they work to provide the care, but somehow the tasks that they learned to perform so well have become completely routine, monotonous, and unfulfilling. To save these employees it often takes such efforts as paid time off for personal and professional development, along with the opportunity to redefine the nature of the job itself to make it more challenging and growth promoting.

There are, however, jobs that fit the team player profile and people who seem to be content to perform those jobs indefinitely as long as they feel part of the group and that they are contributing to the overall effort of the company. Peter Vaill describes this situation as "the retention of an abstract commitment to the task, even if concretely one's heart is not in it" (1989, p. 68).

I remember a conversation years ago with Mildred, a member of a maintenance crew in my building at the university. I pointed out how incredibly clean the place always looked, especially in comparison to other buildings on campus. Her response was that it was important to all members of the crew to maintain "a really nice place for these kids to go to school." I asked her how she liked doing the same job day after day. She said, "It's not important for me to like the work as long as the place always looks clean. Besides, we (the crew) have some fun while we do our job."

Organizations are filled with people like Mildred. Unfortunately, they are the ones who are easily taken for granted because they never complain, they are highly dependable, and there is no obvious reason to be concerned. Whether an employer should leave well enough alone is not easily decided. If the Mildreds of the world do not ask for change and seem to be in all other respects content with their work lives, perhaps it is best to leave things as they are. However, there seems to be an increasing number of jobs best done by some automated means because they are not tasks that meet human needs. Where these jobs can be done robotically or where they can be redesigned to be more meaningful and intrinsically rewarding to people, such efforts may be worth the investment in the long run.

Figure 8.5. Team Players

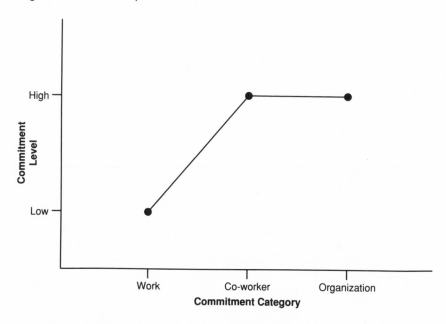

The Overqualified Employee. The following scenario illustrates the classic case of the bright, overqualified employee. A counseling center at a large university had a habit of hiring receptionists who were interested in the work of the center, tended to have values that fit in with the professional members', and who were sensitive and competent. In all cases the individuals started out with high levels of job commitment, but eventually became bored with the routine aspects of the work. At the same time they came to identify strongly with the members of the center and with the purposes served by it. In some instances the receptionist eventually was trained to be a paraprofessional, and in other cases the individual went back to school to obtain the training and degree needed to become a professional. The outcomes represented effective solutions to the problems, but most organizations cannot so easily provide such options. What do you do with someone who is bored with a job, but feels highly committed to the people and the organization?

If it is a repeated problem, the hiring and job-individual matching practices ought to be reviewed. Or, if possible, it may be necessary to redefine the job to make it a better fit for the kinds of people being hired.

One insurance company, for example, had exactly this kind of problem in its sales department: A number of very bright secretaries wanted to be more than secretaries. Rather than lose them or replace them with less intelligent and less dedicated people, the department redefined several positions as "sales assistants" and gave the individuals opportunities and responsibilities to do sales follow-ups and to carry through on contacts initiated by senior sales people. The commitment to their work went up, and the performance of the department improved visibly. Furthermore, the overall sense of team commitment was enhanced through the interactions and successes achieved.

Social Bonders

Although a cohesive work group usually is thought to be a valuable asset to an organization, there are times when the cohesiveness is more related to social needs than the tasks at hand. I refer to the members of such a group as *social bonders*. The performance level of such groups tends to be mediocre at best, usually enough to keep management from dissolving the group or firing individuals. The real problem with this situation is that a highly cohesive group whose norms are counter to the goals of the organization can be a real obstacle to the firm's success. The social bonding maintains the group, but may or may not serve task objectives (see Figure 8.6). In some respects the bonding can be functional in the sense that it can help minimize turnover and absenteeism, and it may even keep people working in jobs that are inherently unfulfilling and for organizations that do not engender much commitment. However, since the quality of the work tends to be poor, socially bonded groups can damage the organization's total work effort.

Figure 8.6. Social Bonders

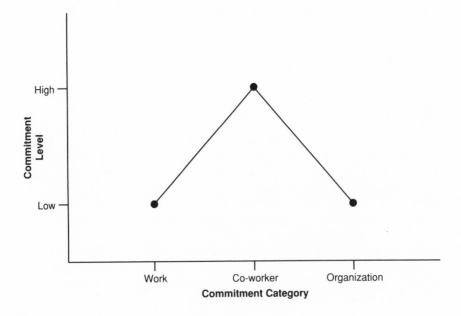

Many traditional managers are ready to assume that employees would rather socialize than work: social bonders only confirm that assumption. When commitment to work and to the organization are low and interpersonal commitment is high, it is not unreasonable to assume that employees would much rather socialize than work. The employees, as a group, put in at least minimal effort to protect the group, but much more than that seems difficult to obtain. Consequently, managers are more likely to break up the social bonders, thus destroying the last remnants of commitment, than to seek ways to build commitment to the work and the organization, using the existing co-worker commitment as a foundation. The example that follows illustrates how this kind of situation can be turned around.

The Hospital Dietary Department. A dietary department in a large hospital faced a serious problem with many of its employees. Their jobs involved distributing meals to patients, most of whom were chronically disabled, and collecting the food trays after the meals. The tasks were routine and carefully structured so that all employees carried out the procedures in exactly the same way. The inevitable boredom affected the attitudes that the employees brought with them to the patients' rooms. They did not especially like the work, and they did not see the value of their efforts in relation to the goals of the hospital. However, they did enjoy each other's company and took advantage of every opportunity to socialize, often at the expense of the work.

Firing employees was not a good option because it was difficult to replace them even at that level of work. Coming down hard with threats of disciplinary action tended to make matters worse because disgruntled, resentful employees were not good for the patients.

I was employed as a psychologist in that hospital, and I was asked to consult on the problem. Although I did not define it then in terms of commitment per se, I did suggest some actions that were consistent with the principles reflected in this book. I suggested and helped implement an educational approach in which the dietary personnel were given a series of seminars on the kinds of illnesses being treated at the hospital, the kind of medical and nursing care needed, and the ways in which nutrition was a key factor in the recovery of patients. The sessions were conducted by the medical and nursing staff and, at times, involved bringing patients into the classroom to talk with participants.

The educational process provided the employees with valuable information and helped them identify with total patient care, which was the principal goal of the hospital. Furthermore, they began to see themselves as important to the professional staff and not just to the maintenance of their own peer groups. Over time their commitment to performing their jobs well increased noticeably in both behavior and attitude. They took more responsibility to see to it that patients were fed and even performed special favors for patients whenever possible.

This approach generated identification with organizational mission, which in turn made the otherwise routine work more meaningful. In looking back I think more could have been done to increase commitment to the task itself (the delivery of meals to the patients and the picking up of trays). There were occasional examples of employees who would decorate a tray with flowers or arrange the food in some special way, lending a personal touch. This behavior could have been encouraged more and even broadened to permit employees to cater to some of the personal desires of patients.

It was fortunate that the seminars alleviated much of the problem, but it required a continuing effort and time from the medical staff. However, one of the most important aspects of the seminars was that they brought the employees together in the very groups with which they already identified and introduced new content. Consequently, the peer group began to relate more and more to hospital work and not just to social relationships. The net result was that employee identification with organizational goals was reinforced by both the formal classroom sessions and the informal interactions outside the classroom.

Good Soldiers

The *good soldiers* of an organization very often are so far from the mainstream of activities spiritually that management tends to forget that they are around, although they may be performing functions quite vital to more obvious organizational purposes. This situation is more common than many managers realize. It is typified by long-time employees who tend to work alone on jobs that have minimal intrinsic interest or challenge. The tasks are usually routine, but may be essential to the core operation or maintenance of the organization (see Figure 8.7). What keeps the employee putting forth effort to do a good job is a belief in the purposes of the organization. Although this may be accompanied by a strong work ethic, the distinguishing feature is the employee's strong identification with the organization itself.

Many first generation European immigrants were in such jobs, often far below their abilities. Companies that would hire them were seen as "good" companies, and the workers eventually developed a strong sense of pride in working there, even in menial jobs.

Again, managers can take good soldiers for granted; they do not create problems, and they can be highly reliable. But the long-term effects might not be as positive as they could be if management were more creative in tapping the talents of these employees. For example, a group of dedicated veterans just might come up with some useful ideas for improving the ways in which work is carried out. This kind of involvement can be a powerful means of generating both work and co-worker identification, and it might prevent the existing level of commitment to the organization from dying off altogether.

Figure 8.7. Good Soldiers

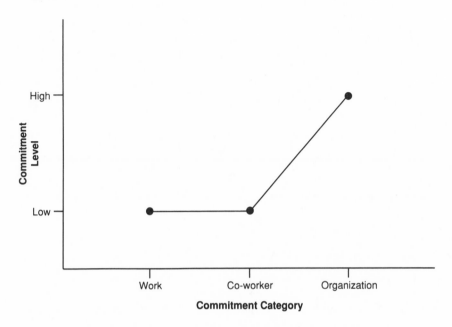

The Mail Clerk. I once talked to a mail clerk who had been at his job for more than thirty years, but never stopped doing his best in the routine task of sorting mail into appropriate boxes. When I asked him if he ever got bored, he said he did most of the time. When I asked him why he did not talk much with other mail workers, he said that he never had much to say to them. When I asked him why he never slacked off or slowed down, he said he always believed that the ability of people to reach each other across many miles is one of the most important things in this life. In his mind, the mail did this better than anything.

This man felt that he was making a difference and that he was part of an organization that was doing something valuable, something with which he could identify. In his case that was probably enough. It may not be enough for other people, those who often are overlooked until perhaps a special ceremony is held to honor them for years of dedicated service.

One might wonder whether to leave well enough alone. The same commitment and performance probably will continue for many more years. But why not build on that person's dedication in ways that can serve both the organization and the individual? Such an employee probably embodies many of the values and cultural norms the company should foster. Most jobs can be enriched and improved or even redesigned to be more challenging. And who knows the job more intimately than someone who has done it for many years? It is wise to take advantage of this whenever possible. Even jobs that look like they cannot be redesigned turn out to be readily modifiable upon a closer look.

Furthermore, if one convenes a group of these dedicated veterans to look at ways of improving several aspects of the work, some strong team identification and spirit may develop. It is valuable to take advantage of untapped human resources, especially in employees who quietly do their jobs, never complain, and therefore tend to fade into the background.

Finally, it is important for a manager to stay open to the possibility that these unsung heroes usually look to top management to change things. They maintain high production from a belief in the system (commitment), but much of their day-to-day behavior is governed by habit (compliance). Initiative on a manager's part might prevent whatever commitment is left from dying off.

Defeated Players

If employees feel little or no identification with their work, co-workers, and the organization, they can be described as *defeated players* (see Figure 8.8). If this is widespread, the organization may be described as a *defeated system,* one that has lost many of its productive people, is struggling to maintain at least minimal performance from those who remain, and has become so self-protective and defensive that it cannot solve problems effectively. It exhibits low morale to the point of depression, often casts blame on outside forces or inside scapegoats, and has lost faith in its own leaders, even those who could, if given the chance, turn things around.

The defeated system has become increasingly familiar in recent years, given the turbulence of the economy and the changing international scene. New organizational views and innovative leadership will be required for many corporations to meet the challenges inherent in the future. We are faced with an era of "permanent white water," as Peter Vaill so aptly stated in *Managing as a Performing Art* (1989).

Rejuvenating defeated players is difficult even when the problem is not widespread in the organization. Usually, it requires such efforts as major job changes, extended leaves for educational pursuits, and perhaps even whole new careers for employees. The situation often results in an individual leaving the organization altogether.

However, that does not have to happen. Many companies are becoming more flexible in their attitudes and policies about creating opportunities for career changes within the system, especially as traditional "stovepipe" structures are replaced by more flexible and open forms. Willingness to provide a variety of career options can prevent an organization from having too many defeated players and risking becoming a defeated system.

Figure 8.8. Defeated Players

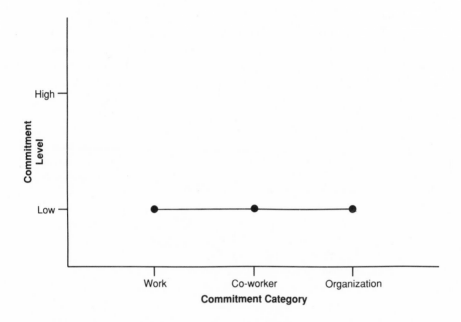

One irony of a defeated system is that it is in such a survival mode that management focuses on short-term financial issues, usually cost containment, when what is needed most is a creative exploration of long-term strategy. Unfortunately, the long-term strategy is counter to the natural tendency of people under stress. The focus tends to be on ways to reduce the tension and not on ways to manage the uncertainty of the future. Furthermore, the internal dynamics of the system tend to be control oriented, thus inhibiting creative ideas. Information that should be shared tends to be guarded, and individuals and groups find themselves competing for scarce resources instead of collaborating in the best interests of the organization as a whole.

While a conscious and deliberate choice to dissolve the system is sometimes the only and perhaps best option, and although the picture can seem terminally bleak, there are ways to turn such situations around. An example is described in the next section, but suffice it to say at this point that most organizations do learn how to come out of major crises intact, and many learn valuable lessons. However, survival necessarily begins with an acknowledgment of reality and a willingness to take ownership of the situation and all its problems. A further discussion of crisis management is presented in Chapter 12.

The Oil Company Division. Three years prior to my arrival as a consultant, the petrochemicals division of a large oil company had begun a new venture: to establish, within three years, a profitable operation in a highly competitive market for petrochemical products. The entire division was like a team with a mission, and all members were excited about it.

By the end of the three years, the division had failed to meet its objectives; management and employees were experiencing a major sense of defeat. Any sense of purpose had disappeared, individuals were looking out for themselves, and the work seemed meaningless and empty. What had happened was that the division had found itself more and more constrained—and literally sabotaged—by control from headquarters. Because of red tape, it repeatedly lost opportunities to respond quickly to market opportunities. The division found itself lacking the authority to make the decisions that would have enabled it to compete effectively. The entrepreneurial spirit had been squashed by the weight of the larger organization's policy and control. One result was a group of defeated players at the top of the division.

How does one turn this situation around? Clearly it cannot be done by "treating" the division and not its parent. The birth of the division showed the ingredients that generate a high level of commitment, ingredients related to all three kinds of identification. But trying to rekindle the fires of that commitment would be quite difficult because of the current realities and the three-year history. Even if successful, history was bound to repeat itself unless the overall system were to change its way of managing entrepreneurial subunits.

What actually happened was that the division managers, after a series of extended meetings with corporate officers, were able to renegotiate decision-making authority and, consequently, turn things around for a time. Spirits rose, teamwork was renewed, and a sense of a winning team emerged again— but only for awhile. Organization policies allowed people to be moved around like chess pieces. Within a year, many of the key people in the management team had been replaced, without attention to maintenance of the team effort, and more and more people slipped back to a self-serving style. The sense of common purpose again was gone, illustrating how an effective system needs to institutionalize its effectiveness, not let it depend upon the presence of a particular cast of characters.

Using the Profiles for Diagnosis

Table 8.1 summarizes the eight commitment profiles, including typical problems or "symptoms" found in each, and suggests interventions. It is not meant to be an all-inclusive body of information, but to illustrate ways to use the profiles for diagnosis.

Fitting Profiles to Situations

System Performers. In today's rapidly growing and ever-changing organizations, where uncertainty prevails and external competition runs high, truly

Table 8.1

Commitment Profiles, Characteristics, and Interventions

Profile	Characteristics	Interventions
System Performers	High individual performance; cohesive teams; intergroup co-operation; organizational focus.	Continuous recognition and celebration; do not become complacent.
Team Performers	High individual performance; cohesive teams; tension and conflict between groups.	Require cross-group interactions with common goals; increase lateral integration.
Contributing Performers	High individual performance; poor teamwork; focus on one's own relationship with organization.	Team building; train managers in group process skills.
Individualistic Performers	High individual performance; indifference to team and total organization.	Establish team centered rewards; link personal career goals to organizational goals.
Team Players	Moderate level of performance to maintain group membership and keep job.	Job enrichment; improve match between job and employee.
Social Bonders	Poor to moderate performance; strong social norms; weak task norms.	Build on cohesiveness by having group redesign its work to fit organizational objectives.

Table 8.1
Commitment Profiles, Characteristics, and Interventions (continued)

Good Soldiers	Adequate level of performance; low interest in job or co-workers; only concern is the good of the organization.	Redesign work to add variety and challenge; where possible, utilize team structure.
Defeated Players	Low performance; low morale; high level of tension and uncertainty; people abandoning ship.	Gather data on a system-wide basis; create and implement long-term organization development effort.

successful enterprises will be populated with system performers. These organizations will rely heavily on the commitment of their employees to perform at their best, produce quality products and service, and do them from an internalized dedication to a common purpose. Compliance will not do the job, nor will commitment at a local level. Real success will require people who identify with all aspects of their work, including their co-workers and the total system.

It may be difficult to know at the time of hiring just how well an individual fits the profile, but an interview often provides a sense of the person's beliefs or values related to work, co-worker relationships, and the goals of the organization. Certainly as time goes on an observant manager can be aware of the different commitment indicators reflected in the employee's behavior and attitudes. If there is a serious concern about employees, a more systematic assessment, even something as formal as the CDI, can be useful for identifying patterns of commitment. Finally, paying attention to the kinds of problems or symptoms in Table 8.1 can be an effective way to determine a course of action to improve commitment.

While system performers seem to be the ideal employees and defeated players not, several other profiles can be appropriate for different situations and for certain kinds of organizations.

Team Performers. Team performers are suited to organizations in which team activities tend to be self-contained, where little or no interdependence between or among teams is necessary. Although it might be desirable for team members to identify with the total organization anyway, strong identification with work and with co-workers on the team is much more essential. Research project teams, for example, can serve the organization very well as long as the special talents of the members are devoted to the work and the members can work well together.

However, it can be important for management to look ahead to future changes in the organizational interdependencies. If, for example, it can be anticipated that new projects might involve collaboration across existing team boundaries, it would be wise to plant the seeds for those relationships as early as possible, which would help keep organizational priorities above team priorities.

Contributing Performers. Contributing performers work well in jobs that involve little interpersonal, especially group-centered, activity, but which do require employees to work to attain their own goals and to act in the best interests of the organization's goals. The example given earlier of a company made up of a large and dispersed sales force, with each salesperson operating individually, probably needs contributing performers more than system performers. It might be satisfied with individualistic performers on a short-term basis, but if turnover is a concern, that profile is not suitable. Also, if the company wants its sales people to be effective ambassadors for the organization (good representatives of its desired image and reputation), the contributing performer clearly is the preferred profile.

Here again the wise manager looks ahead to changes that may occur in the way work is carried out. With trends toward team activities increasing, it is possible that tasks that currently rely solely upon the efforts of the individual might eventually be restructured around teams. That is already happening in companies that have sales functions that are organized by product lines or geographic regions and where all sales personnel are held responsible for sales in a given area. Instead of individual effort alone, it usually takes a team effort to achieve success. In this case contributing performers need to become system performers.

Individualistic Performers. Temporary help, particularly highly skilled technical or professional people, usually perform well if they are committed to their work. Identification with co-workers or the organization tends to be of little importance for the period of employment. Although compliance with job requirements may be acceptable for that period, commitment to the work becomes increasingly important to the extent that the employee has to work independently and exercise some degree of professional judgment. Although temporary employees usually are hired on the basis of skills alone, it is worth a manager's time to try to find people who feel an investment and pride in their work, who do not just see it as one more task to be performed in order to make a living.

If there is any chance that a temporary employee will be hired on a permanent basis or even for an extended period, it can be valuable to foster that person's identification with co-workers and the organization. That kind of effort also helps prevent the development of a status system in which the employee is treated as less important and less legitimate than others doing similar work.

Team Players. Although I would have some concern about the long-term effects of an employee working at something that no longer holds any intrinsic interest, it happens to be one of the realities of many jobs in many organizations. Until the time comes, if it ever does, when most highly monotonous work can be automated or robotized, there will be work that is simply routine, repetitious, and dull. One way to keep people at these jobs and at the same time provide some sources of personal satisfaction is to structure the work around teams. Because the work often does not require skilled supervision, the teams can be self-managing, which serves as an additional source of reward for the group. Team players are ideally suited to these circumstances, since co-worker connectedness and organizational identification serve as the driving forces for the team's efforts.

One of the options that should be kept open with team players, especially if they are working in self-managing teams, is the possibility that they will, because of their existing level of commitment, find ways to improve the way the work is conducted and invent ways to make it more intrinsically challenging. One consequence, should this occur, is that team players eventually will become system players.

Social Bonders. Social bonding alone is not an impetus for performance beyond the minimum. Organizations would not find employees in this category to be acceptable except under extraordinary circumstances. One circumstance might be during a period of major transition or serious crisis, during which there is a great deal of uncertainty about the future, which jobs will be lost, what restructuring might occur, and where employees might end up after things settle down. At such times one of the few things that keeps people from leaving is their sense of social connection to other employees. Social bonders, if they have nothing else to hold them in the organization, have their co-workers. This phenomenon can make a great deal of difference to the ultimate survival of an organization in crisis. However, once the system is operating normally, the other dimensions of commitment, namely work and organization, will require attention if social bonders are ever to become performers.

Good Soldiers. Many jobs are routine and performed in relative isolation. Until organizations can eliminate such jobs, the people who do them best, or at least with the fewest adverse effects, might be individuals who have limited intellectual capacity and who are more comfortable working by themselves than with others. During hard economic times many people are desperate enough to take such jobs, but clearly not out of free choice.

When we consider the good soldiers we find in them the important element of commitment to the organization. Although the work itself is not personally fulfilling or socially rewarding, these employees have made the choice to keep doing something that makes a difference to others. This should not be underestimated, despite the serious shortcomings of other aspects of the job. Because there are jobs that need good soldiers, it is useful to an organization to find those people and to recognize them for their contributions to the organization's goals. It is equally important, however, to seek every opportunity to redesign the work and restructure the social patterns to broaden the basis of commitment beyond the one dimension.

As a final point, I want to suggest that any use of the commitment profiles as a means of matching people to jobs should be considered in the context of change. Jobs change, people change, and organizations change, and not always in predictable or controllable ways. Today's best fit of an employee to a work situation may become tomorrow's worst fit. Insofar as the employees have opportunities to shape and reshape the ways they fit the organization, management can be assured that the levels of commitment associated with any profile will be at their maximum.

Chapter 9

Building Commitment in Individual Employees

From a position of authority or power, it is a lot easier to get compliance from people than commitment. And a manager who tends to focus on immediate results rather than long-term effects might even settle for compliance. The problem is that when people do things because they are afraid of the consequences of *not* doing them, they do not really give their best. In fact, their internal resistance (and often resentment) builds to the point where a supervisor may have to stay on top of them every minute to get them to work. Is this what managers want from their employees—resistance, resentment, mediocre effort? Probably not.

Why do so many managers settle for compliance rather than make an effort to get commitment from their employees? From my conversations with a variety of managers it seems that there are many answers, but the ones that stand out are illustrated by these responses:

- "I'm not sure I can trust them to get the work done."
- "They probably won't do it the way I want them to."
- "I'm held accountable, and I can't afford to have them make a mistake."
- "I think they need my help and supervision."
- "I don't seem to know how to get them to be more committed."

Let us take a look at each answer to see if there is some way to deal with the issues and avoid the traps.

Trusting Employees

Managers have discovered that they often get from their employees what they expect to get. Douglas McGregor pointed this out years ago when he drew the distinction between Theory X and Theory Y assumptions (McGregor,

1960). Without going into detail, the essence of what McGregor said is that if managers assume that people are naturally lazy and do not want to work, they tend to exercise tight control, watching every minute of employees' time, which produces resentment and low interest in the work. That he called Theory X. If, however, managers assume that people are naturally inclined to work, managers will tend to use opportunities to give employees more responsibility and not watch their every move, which usually results in higher productivity (though not always) and better morale (almost always). That he called Theory Y. Theory Y is built on trust and Theory X on direct control.

One benefit of having a high level of commitment in employees is that they usually can be counted on to carry through on tasks even in the manager's absence. But for that to occur control must be shared with them. A manager who retains it does not allow people the opportunity to act on their commitment to the boss, the job, or the organization. Sometimes it is hard to let go of control, especially when times are difficult and pressure from the top is strong. But managers who delegate decisions and responsibility to committed employees ultimately find that their own sense of control actually increases, employees' levels of commitment increase, and the managers' freedom to attend to high priority matters and to just think clearly about the future are enhanced.

Trusting employees to do their best work in one's absence can seem risky at times. If the right people are on the job, it really is not so risky. If not, it is time to review hiring practices. But usually, especially with new employees, one must take a risk at some point. And most of the time, willingness to do so pays off. Most people do not want to stand still in their work or in their lives, for that matter; they want the chance to stretch and grow. Therefore, they want to be trusted in their work. When trusted they become committed; they internalize the value of the work and its related goals. Furthermore, they are likely to identify with, and later emulate, their boss, the person who trusted them in the first place. The payoff can be considerable for the employee, the boss, and the organization.

There is a self-fulfilling prophecy at work in all this. Treat people as though they are lazy and they somehow become lazy; treat them as though they are responsible and they usually live up to it. Of course, some Theory X types do not live up to Theory Y assumptions. A manager who can live with that will find it a small price to pay for the sustained commitment of the majority of employees.

There are some simple steps that can move a Theory X situation to a Theory Y situation. Begin by negotiating a contract with each employee. Make the expectations of each other clear, including an agreement that if things change or the expectations prove to be unrealistic, one or the other will initiate a renegotiation. This approach can help avoid the trap of making global assumptions (X or Y) about employees. Rather, it allows an opportunity to see each as an individual operating along a continuum from X to Y, which even changes over time with respect to the need for supervision and the ability to take on increasing responsibility.

The one-on-one contact enhances a manager's personal impact; the opportunity for employees to negotiate their own work expectations increases the degree to which they will internalize and identify with the work and the goals of the organization.

Is Loyalty a Dying Concept?

In a fit of nostalgia a long-time manager might look back on the old days longingly, wondering what ever happened to "employee loyalty." Of course, those days tend to look better at a distance than up close. The fact is, loyalty is not dead at all; it simply stems from sources other than those that generated it forty or fifty (or more) years ago. It is no longer blind allegiance or even informed allegiance to authority, to leadership, or to a single principle—it no longer can depend on compliance in any form. It depends much more on informed free choice. As discussed earlier, the so-called loyalty was more the result of a transaction and not necessarily genuine commitment, while commitment emerges from managerial practices that empower employees to fulfill their potential.

At one time identification with a powerful organizational leader was enough to inspire loyalty, but today it seems the identification must go beyond the leader and include active involvement, participation, and ownership with respect to the goals of the organization. Now organizational leaders must actively *share* their visions by creating ways to move them into the very fibers of their organizations. That is not easy to do, especially for those managers who deal with day-to-day or moment-to-moment operations.

In fact, some visionary leaders generate terrible conflicts in their organizations because their strengths as visionaries seem to preclude awareness of day-to-day problems, some of which occur *because* of the lack of awareness. Thus, they may inspire commitment in those close to them, but they fail to give adequate attention to those on the front lines.

Typical of this pattern are entrepreneurs who have built exciting, growing enterprises and do not know their own limits in the management of those enterprises, especially when they grow beyond some critical size. The very person whose vision inspired in others the commitment to build the system becomes an obstacle to those whose work lives are more related to short-run objectives and performance. Their commitment depends upon identification with the work and with co-workers more than with the blue-sky vision of the organization's creator. This is not to say that identification with visionary leadership and company mission are not important; it is only to point out that the leader's original vision usually is not enough to sustain commitment in the absence of work and peer identification.

An entrepreneur with a vision must share that vision with everyone concerned. An entrepreneur who is not good at managing the linear operations of the firm must get out of the way and let others do it—and be sure to give them the authority and resources necessary.

Freedom on the Job

Chances are every job can be tackled in a variety of ways. While some are tightly constrained by technology, most have some degree of freedom. That one way has worked well for one person does not mean it will work well for others. But it is often difficult to believe that another way may be just as good because it may burst a little bubble in the ego.

I knew one manager at an insurance company who seemed to have compulsion to correct anything and everything done by those who reported directly to him, even when the corrections were trivial and often totally unnecessary. He said he was aware of this, but could not help himself because he really believed he could always do something better than the next person or could always improve on whatever someone else did. His behavior demoralized his employees and seemed to result only in an increase in errors on their part, which the manager had to correct, and which served to justify his behavior in the first place.

In *Zen and the Art of Motorcycle Maintenance* (1974), Robert Pirsig views life as a set (or many sets) of interrelated forces, concepts, and ideas. The author describes the engine of the motorcycle (used both literally and figuratively) as a complex network of interrelated forces that move in concert to produce an effect, namely the power to move the bike. Most repair manuals are step-by-step procedures that define a lock-step sequence of events rather than a total configuration that can be understood from many perspectives.

Most large scale work efforts are also complex networks of forces that can be best understood as configurations with many perspectives, not as lock-step procedures or activities that move in a linear fashion. The assembly of a piece of equipment, the provision of certain kinds of medical care, or the learning of many types of subject matter in school requires that some steps precede others. But the thinking and planning activities allow room for each person's own personal style. And that style can give greater meaning to the work and, thus, enhance one's identification with it.

The assembly workers at Saab-Scandia back in 1969 were given the opportunity to develop their own way of doing things in teams that took responsibility for the quantity and quality of their work. What the workers did (build cars) was not a matter for self-determination; how they did it, within some limits, was left for them to determine. In many instances worker teams have been known to put their names on the cars they assembled. That kind of action, it seems, reflects internalized work values.

By building on the sociotechnical thinking that shaped the Saab efforts, there are some steps one can take to get away from having employees doing things exclusively one way.

First, make sure everyone understands the purely technical aspects of the job that has to be done and also that everyone understands it in the same way.

Second, analyze the behavioral aspects of the task, and even the social aspects for jobs that require cooperation among employees. One usually discovers that while one has certain behavioral and social preferences, there is usually room for variation without changing any of the technical aspects of the job. This is especially true in white collar work and in the complex activities characteristic of high tech industry.

Third, it is important to establish with employees a *mutual* understanding of the technical and behavioral/social aspects of the work and use it to negotiate how the work is to be conducted.

New employees may be more than happy to do it the manager's way at first, but watch for cues that say it is time to renegotiate that agreement. Learning and growth mean increased self-determination. Managers who can respect that process and support it in their employees foster their commitment. In addition, the manager becomes a role model for identification and creates conditions in which people can merge their personal styles with their work, thus identifying with the work itself.

Sharing Accountability

Certainly the buck stops with the manager, but what is there to prevent sharing "the buck"? We *are* accountable for what we do or do not do in our jobs, as well as for the successes and failures of the people who work for us. The irony is that when one feels the pressure most, that is the time one needs employee commitment the most, yet it is also when one is inclined to be self-protective, not share information openly, convey tension and anxiety to others, and, in general, engage in the kind of overcontrolling behavior that makes the situation worse. When employees know that the boss is afraid, they often make mistakes, not intentionally (we hope) but out of their own tension and anxiety.

People almost always respond favorably to the opportunity to share the load with someone they respect or admire. Of course, managers may not be certain of the extent to which employees respect or admire them, but they need to start somewhere. Sharing responsibility through delegation conveys a sense of trust, which fosters a willingness or even eagerness to live up to the trust. Under such circumstances it is the best employees who want to give careful attention to the work and really watch out for mistakes.

If one responds to the pressure of accountability by overcontrolling employees and treating them like irresponsible children, they will become confused as to why the boss is behaving that way, and they will be more inclined to resist than to be supportive. Share the problem; share the pressure. Give them a chance to come through. Their willingness to put in whatever time and effort it takes to keep things going, to keep productivity, service, and quality at the maximum may be surprising. A manager who is willing to do this in times of stress, when it is most difficult, will find that his or her own tolerance for the stress will increase. (Chapter 12 looks at the problems related to stress in times of crisis.) In addition, the ownership of successes and failures will be shared and vitality and commitment will be reflected in the behavior and attitudes of employees.

Help and Supervision

When we are struggling with something new and unfamiliar, we may want help but we probably do not want the task completely taken over by another person. It is possible to help someone too much. Most managers feel it is their responsibility to help and supervise their employees. No doubt this is a key part of being an effective manager. Unfortunately, many do not know what helping someone means. Instead of allowing the person needing help to define the kind of help needed, the helper all too often decides it instead. The result may or may not be the provision of real help.

Remember when our parents helped us with our homework? Did they let us struggle a bit until we mastered something, or did they get so worried about our doing well that they actually took over the task themselves? It is not very different with employees. Learning and mastering new skills can require some struggle and frustration; without the struggle and frustration there may be little satisfaction or real learning. Besides, don't we feel a stronger commitment to something for which we worked hard than if something is handed to us?

Supervision involves similar considerations. Again, newer workers usually want to become oriented in how to do things properly and may be quite explicit about wanting supervision, at least initially. But do not supervise where it is not needed. Check out whether one's being around or dropping in is perceived as an act of support (which is fine) or an attempt to check up on people (which may not be).

It is important to check this out directly because one could err in the wrong direction. In eagerness *not* to exercise unnecessary supervision one might become so distant that employees wonder if the boss really cares about what they are doing. It is a fine line to tread, and it may seem impossible. However, a manager who is open and direct about intentions reinforces that same openness in others, gives and receives the correct message more clearly.

Again it is a matter of negotiation from the start. If one knows one's tendencies (and one should to be effective), let employees know them also. For example, if managers know they have strong control needs and tend to help too much or oversupervise, they should give their employees permission to call them on it and to define their own limits. Managers must be sure the employees test them on that permission and that they honor it. If, on the other hand, managers tend to be reticent about offering help or in acting in a supervisory capacity, they must give employees permission to ask for help and to demand attention and supervision. And managers must be sure the employees do it and it is honored.

These negotiations do not come easily at first. In fact, some employees initially may be puzzled by them. However, it is important to give it a chance. The kind of reciprocal support that results can be well worth the effort. Employees will find it rewarding and are likely to do it themselves with their subordinates. In this case the resulting commitment will extend beyond the work to the people involved in it.

Generating Commitment through One's Own Behavior

I already have covered some of the most important ways to generate commitment—building trust, letting people develop their own ways to work, sharing accountability and ownership of a job, and negotiating help and supervision in terms that engender employee development. Now I would like to give special attention to two aspects of managerial behavior that can have powerful effects on the degree to which others identify with the boss, their work, and the organization. In the first place managers need to be *role models,* by being committed. Second, managers need to *empower* others in their jobs and roles.

Being a Role Model

If one is not committed to what one is doing, to the people in the organization or to its mission, it will be very difficult to generate commitment in others. One is likely to reduce the level of energy and be a poor role model. This first step is perhaps the most critical one because a careful self-examination might lead one to make a major change in one's job, career, or place of employment.

We will assume for the sake of argument that one is reasonably committed to one's work, the people there, and to the organization. It means that one can honestly say to oneself, "I'm not just complying out of fear, blind loyalty, ignorance, or anything else; I believe in what this organization is all about (its mission), and I experience a sense of satisfaction and worth in the job I perform." Now ask whether others can *see* that commitment. Do they see a boss who shows enthusiasm and even joy in the work? Or is the boss so caught up in details, procedures, pressures, and the like that people see only a harried, worried boss who would be happier someplace else?

People take their cues from the top. Chances are good that much of the behavior of employees is a reflection of the boss's behavior. Even without asking, it might be possible to get some idea of one's own impact by watching subordinates. Some of the commitment indicators can be useful here. For example, if they are enthusiastic, chances are they see the boss as enthusiastic; if they appear sullen and tense, one probably can assume that at least some of those feelings are being picked up from the boss.

One may discover that one needs to develop a clear sense of purpose or vision with which people can identify. The vision gives one focus, which generates energy and creates a rallying point for the energies of others.

Importance of Accessibility and Predictability in the Boss. No two factors in a relationship hold more potential power than *accessibility* and *predictability*. A person in a position to control important resources (money, information, permission) can exercise power negatively or positively. If that person makes the resources inaccessible, it may prevent people from doing their jobs, which demonstrates how much power that person has, but may also reduce their commitment to the boss and often to their jobs. Who has not worked for a boss who did the disappearing act at the most inopportune times? It does not do much for one's blood pressure, and often the subordinate ends up being blamed for whatever went wrong. Managers who control a resource that others need must make it and themselves accessible: it facilitates getting the job done and, central to our concern here, builds commitment in those who depend on them.

The other factor, *predictability,* may be harder to control. In the normal chaos and craziness of work, we all look for some sources of stability and consistency. A boss whose behavior is erratic, who might say yes to a request on one day and might shout someone out of the room for the same request on another day, is simply not doing much to make life any less hectic and tense. In fact, such behavior can produce such incredible tension that it may lead people to avoid the boss as much as possible. That will not do much to enhance commitment to either the boss or to the work.

Moody bosses should try to let employees know when they will and will not be receptive to requests for information or approval. Bosses who are not sure whether they are perceived as unpredictable (which is really what determines other people's behavior) would do well to check it out. They could ask those who have known them the longest and who may be willing to be most open with them. But keep in mind that if people do perceive the supervisor as unpredictable, they might be very hesitant to be honest, for fear of getting the unpleasant reaction. It is possible to get around that dilemma by being open, by acknowledging one's awareness and concern about the impact of one's behavior on others. Bosses who succeed in changing their personal power from negative to positive see a visible difference in the performance and attitudes of their employees.

Empower Others

It is not enough for the boss alone to have a vision of the future or a sense of overall mission; it must be shared with others so that they can identify with it. The process of sharing empowers others to work in the same direction, toward the same ends. To accomplish this one needs to create:

- Shared beliefs,
- Shared ownership of goals,
- Personal connections to goals and values, and
- Opportunities for employees to design and control their own work.

Shared Beliefs. The "We can do it!" slogan of the Mary Kay organization provides a powerful rallying cry for its employees. It is shared and internalized by everyone in the company, whose success has been noteworthy.

I do not advocate a slogan for everyone or gathering employees in a huddle and clasping hands. But I do suggest that a successful enterprise depends upon spirit, and spirit comes from beliefs. If the beliefs are enthusiastically shared and supported by individuals, they feel empowered to devote energy to a successful outcome. If one's vision and beliefs in what one is trying to accomplish are shared with only a few close colleagues, one will never bring out the full potential of employees. Entrusting a piece of oneself to others brings back returns multiplied many times over.

A department head needs to develop a sense of purpose or mission for the department relative to the overall purposes of the organization. Where does one want to take the department in the next six months or even the next two years? What kind of a place does one want it to be? How does one want people who are part of the department to feel and behave? How far can one go in both the quantity and quality of the work? By stopping and asking these questions and discussing them and generating consensual answers, one is well on the way to creating a shared set of beliefs for the unit—whether it is a department, a project team, a committee, or a strategic planning group. It is amazing just how energized people can get just from sharing a vision and beliefs. And that energy takes the form of a joint commitment to the work, each other, and the organization.

I have noticed that many approaches to organizational change have lost the original vision that inspired them and have become buried in the techniques and mechanics of implementation. A typical example is in the area of service excellence, which fundamentally is a philosophical set of beliefs about the best way to conduct business. When people internalize that philosophy and behave in ways that reflect it, the effects are powerful and long lasting. Unfortunately, many organizations eager to provide quality service (or products) institute training programs that focus on techniques intended to get them there in a hurry. The time needed to really internalize the philosophy and live by it is measurable at least in months, but more often in years. Unfortunately, many managers who seek immediate results are disappointed. What may have started out as a valid and substantive approach to organizational improvement has, in many cases, become distilled to the point of becoming a fad.

Shared Ownership of Goals. This step and the next are logical extensions of the first. Goals relate to the outcomes of tasks, and tasks usually are subdivided in ways that separate individuals from one another—and appropriately so. However, if all members of a group feel some ownership of (a stake in) the overall the goals of the group, the separate goals will not become forces that divide but those that unite. Some data obtained from the CDI demonstrated just how difficult it can be to get people to appreciate their interdependencies, to not live by a "mind your own business" creed, and to be willing to let their own priorities be subordinated to the needs of the system.

It is important to recognize that goals can be very specific and immediate or very general and long range. The short-term, specific goals are the means by which people monitor their success. Joint success produces cohesiveness and reinforces joint ownership. Furthermore, joint success helps keep people focused on the common, long-range goals and helps sustain commitment to them. When that joint success occurs on an organizational level, the strength of commitment at that level increases.

In short, the shared vision and beliefs alone are not enough to sustain identification with the organization. It is vital to experience a shared success in achieving the goals that move people toward the vision; those goals take on meaning when people feel ownership of them.

Personal Connection to Goals and Values. This is different from ownership. The personal connection occurs when one can say that what one wants to achieve for oneself is the same as what the organization is trying to achieve. We bring this with us into the job. If one's particular competencies and goals are realized through work, the organization need not worry about identification with the job. It is a given. Employees at all levels are empowered by virtue of the assigned work naturally fitting them. It becomes a strong foundation for building shared beliefs and shared ownership of goals.

For managers, it is important to try to maximize the fit between individual goals and organizational goals. It does indeed empower people in their work. The larger the gap in that fit, the more difficult it will be to create shared ownership of goals or vision; the personal connection will be missing.

Identification can be related to many aspects of an individual. If work, for example, is just a means to an end (security, advancement, or self-fulfillment) identification is not nearly as deep or strong as it would be if the work were a reflection of a basic set of values. In any given occupation or profession there is a wide range in the strength of job identification. We know the difference between physicians who are dedicated to their profession (a matter of values) and those who just make a living from it. The difference in workmanship is visible when comparing a carpenter who is an artisan with one who is a nail-pounder. Clearly, greater commitment can be expected from people who perceive their jobs as reflections and extensions of their values, rather than just tasks that they can perform well but primarily serve other ends.

Furthermore, some people see commitment to others as more than instrumental to their own goals: They see it as important in its own right, as a reflection of what is "good" or "right" in life. A violation of a personal commitment, at work or anywhere, is unacceptable and unprofessional. If this type of identification extends to the purpose or mission of the organization as a whole, people experience membership in and opportunities to contribute to that organization as powerful reinforcements of their own basic values.

Then there are value conflicts. While one might compromise on goals, values probably are non-negotiable. This does not mean that people do not modify their values as a result of life's experiences; what it means is that people do not give them up easily and certainly not under pressure from others to conform to an opposing set of values.

The choice of the best organizational fit for the individual goes well beyond that person's goals and competencies. It clearly is a matter of fit between personal values and organizational character. Even if managers experience a good fit between themselves and their organizations (there is a strong identification), they need to be sensitive to the potential for conflict between the values of subordinates, especially new hires, and the values embedded in the organization's culture. Where there is such a conflict a manager cannot expect identification with (and consequently commitment to) the organization's mission and purpose. The manager still may find strong job and even interpersonal identification; if those are enough to maintain satisfactory performance, the manager should leave well enough alone.

Some of the profiles discussed in Chapter 8 reflect just this point. Some teams, for example, can be valuable contributors (high in performance) even though the members have little sense of the big picture. Sometimes, however, value conflicts eat away at people to the point where their work suffers, their relationships deteriorate, and they have to leave the system. While not the happiest of outcomes, it may be the only sensible one for all concerned.

Opportunities for Employees to Design and Control Work. Job satisfaction is not the same as job commitment. It is possible to be satisfied with the job, co-workers, and the organization as a whole without feeling any great commitment to them. In fact, it is possible to feel a high level of commitment to the job, people, and organization and still find any or all of them to be sources of frustration. I have met people at all levels of organizations who are very dissatisfied, but whose level of commitment keeps them producing at their best. Burnout often is the final consequence. In any event, it clearly illustrates the independence of satisfaction and commitment. In my own experience, in fact, I have found that many of the employees who express the greatest dissatisfaction with their organization are those who identify most strongly with it. It seems that their frustration stems from their caring, not from a lack of it.

If managers do all they can to create ideal working conditions and challenging jobs for employees, they may generate job satisfaction but not necessarily commitment. If, on the other hand, using a sociotechnical way of thinking, managers give the employees responsibility to design and manage their work, they just may get both satisfaction and commitment. What they would be doing is creating the opportunity for task ownership, for people to make the work more an extension of themselves. In complex tasks there usually is room for a variety of work styles; let the style be a reflection of the people performing the task.

Furthermore, where tasks are related, as most are today, create opportunities for groups or teams of people to negotiate how they will work together, and give them the freedom to experiment, correct mistakes, and learn from their experiences. The shared goals and accomplishments will produce interpersonal commitment along with commitment to the job itself. Job enrichment specialists focus on the individual; what I advocate here is the logical next step, leading to system enrichment.

Consider the following propositions:

- The more a job can be tailored to the needs of the individual, the more that individual will identify with the work.
- The more an individual interacts with others, the greater will be that individual's identification with co-workers.
- The closer the goals and values of an individual are to the mission and purposes of the organization as a whole, the stronger will be that person's identification with the system as a whole.

The effectiveness of the sociotechnical approach to organizational improvement can be attributed to a major extent to its impact on employee commitment to the work, co-workers, and the organization as a whole. But effective managers do not have to rely on the formal and often elaborate diagnostic procedures used by sociotechnical specialists to bring about some of the same changes. Much of it has to do with basic assumptions and philosophy, as well as day-to-day management practices.

The Importance of Career Tracks

An item of singular importance in the CDI referred to the extent to which an employee's own goals are congruent with and fulfilled through the organization's goals. As pointed out in the previous section, this is a determining factor in one's identification with the organization. For many years a job was a job, and an employee simply waited for opportunities for advancement to open up, an often unpredictable event, before paying a lot of attention to anything like a career path. Either it happened or it did not. Few companies had developed a programmatic approach to career planning.

Nowadays the picture is quite different. Enlightened organizations, of which there seem to be an increasing number, are developing very elaborate systems of career pathing, including professional counseling and guidance. However, what is often missing in these approaches is adequate attention to a close match between employees' needs and values and the organization's purposes. It is often assumed that everyone wants, or should want, the same thing in a career, usually a direct path up the ladder. Rarely do we find enough attention paid to alternative paths that reflect more personal aspirations, especially when the aspirations do not fit the familiar pattern of traditional organizational life. What many organizations provide are what I call *career compliance paths* because they are based upon expectations of people other than the users of the paths.

The challenge to management is to design career paths flexible enough and varied enough to accommodate the diversity of interests in the work force today. That is no easy task. However, if the ultimate objective is to build a high commitment system, it is clearly worth the time and effort to build career paths that foster that commitment. The investment will pay the organization back many times over in terms of the sustained quality of its employees and the levels of performance they deliver.

The following are some guidelines to formulating what I call *career commitment paths:*

1. Start with the assumption that what is best for the employee also will be best for the organization. Since this assumption seems to fly in the face of tradition, it may be hard to convince others of its validity. Try anyway.

2. Add the assumption that all paths are movable and can be patterned and repatterned in an infinite variety of ways. It can be expected that there will be many paths that are taken more frequently than others and may, consequently, provide a greater sense of certainty and security than others. However, even those that were once most familiar already are changing dramatically. For example, the change in role from supervisor to team leader clearly has important implications for career pathing, especially for those who had their sights set on promotions to supervisor. Maintaining a great deal of flexibility allows for the kinds of changes that constantly occur in modern organizations, including changes in structure, purposes, and composition of the workforce.

3. Be sure to pay careful attention to the uniqueness of each employee, which means obtaining all information that might affect that individual's career success.

4. Pay attention to the fit between the individual and the job, not just for the next step, but for the overall pattern of steps that might follow. As long as the system is flexible and the options are open, this is not difficult.

5. Make sure the employee plays a key role, if not the dominant role, in the determination of the career path; make sure that employee is fully informed about the options at each stage as well as the opportunities they afford.

6. Finally, but not last, begin the process as early in the employee's career as possible, recognizing that there may be a point of "career readiness," when the employee is beginning to think beyond the job and about a career. Assigning the employee a mentor can be a critical step that determines success or failure.

These guidelines represent more a philosophy than a procedure. Procedures can vary and be specific to an organization. What makes the essential difference in building career paths that are commitment-based is adherence to the basic philosophy, not to the specific steps used to implement that philosophy.

Chapter 10

Building Co-Worker Commitment

Members of a close-knit group—a team that makes some common effort toward a goal—identify with each other. The whole takes priority over the parts; interdependence is recognized and used. For such a network of relationships to develop and be maintained, the members must know each other honestly and deeply—no games, no second-guessing.

There may be no more powerful a force for goal accomplishment in organizations than groups of people, working together, committed to common goals. An effective top level management team is an excellent role model for this type of commitment. When that model is emulated by middle management groups and even workers on the shop floor (e.g., quality circles), there is a basis for building an integrated system, one in which the total organization has a shared sense of purpose and vision that binds together all the parts—groups and individuals.

In contrast, the failure of top managment to operate as a team can easily undermine all efforts at team building at other levels. In one company where I was working with middle managers, one of them complained, "The top guys behave as though they're immune from the team effort which they impose on the rest of us." This person was not saying that a team effort is wrong, but simply that it must be reflected in a commitment to it at the top; otherwise, it is compliance disguised as commitment.

Chapter 12 looks at the issues related to building that kind of total organizational commitment; this chapter looks specifically at the issues of building co-worker commitment, which occurs between people and in groups.

The items in the CDI co-worker category covered two very general constructs, one pertaining to task interdependence and the other to interpersonal bonding and connectedness. Both are vital aspects of co-worker commitment and, as reflected in some of the research results, do not always occur to the same extent in a given context. First we will look at the issue of task interdependence, keeping in mind that it affects the relationship between two individuals or the relationships among the members of any group. In some sense a group can be understood as a network of two-person relationships, so what we understand about one we can easily apply to the other.

Task Interdependence

There are basically three kinds of interdependence: pooled, serial (or serial-order), and reciprocal. Pooled interdependence occurs when two or more workers are carrying out tasks that do not require any exchange of information or materials between them, but each is contributing to the same end. Sales people usually carry out their jobs independently and in parallel, each responsible for the whole task from beginning to end. Only occasionally would they need to check with each other, perhaps when one needs information possessed by the other or when there is training involved.

In the case of serial interdependence, the relationship is important because one worker cannot do the job until the other has completed his or her work. An assembly line is one example; medical procedures that involve diagnosis followed by treatment is another. The steps involved in producing an insurance policy are yet a third. It is easy to see how one worker's failure to perform can directly affect the next worker's performance.

In reciprocal interdependence the relationships are even more complex, since it involves a constant exchange of information or materials or other resources to get the work done. For this kind of interdependence to succeed it takes a keen awareness by all parties of the activities of the others. Furthermore, it takes a willingness of each to give priority to the needs of the group (or of the other person) for the sake of accomplishing the task.

As suggested by some of the research data, our western traditions of minding our own business and getting our own work done before paying attention to that of others are not easily overcome and may be serious obstacles to attaining true interdependence in teams. For pooled interdependence it may be no problem at all; for serial interdependence it can cause some glitches along the way. For reciprocal interdependence it is a very serious matter. Since more and more working relationships and teams involve reciprocal relationships, some major efforts need to be made to educate managers and workers alike to think and behave in some untraditional ways.

To the extent that organizational members perceive their jobs as part of a network of interdependent relationships, efforts to build effective teams will succeed; to the extent that members focus exclusively or primarily on their own jobs to the exclusion of others', efforts to build effective teams will fail.

The presence of the appropriate level of cooperative thinking may be no guarantee that a team succeed, but without it, it is certain the team never will live up to its full potential.

Building Interdependence

As organizations change and restructure, old groupings and alliances get broken up and new ones are formed. These changes affect interpersonal bonds, discussed in the next section, but they also require redefinitions of task interdependence. Employees need to reframe not only their own tasks, but also the context and network of connections of those tasks to the tasks of others. Furthermore, new task relationships may require working across group boundaries that had not been crossed previously.

Building or rebuilding work structures usually cannot wait for the kinds of attitude and emotional changes that occur with changes in interpersonal relationships. Task requirements are immediate; therefore, any aspects of the work that involve a team effort must be put in place relatively quickly. There are several steps that can help accomplish this.

First, identify the nature of the interdependence required for the total task. It might be clearly one type or a blend of types. For example, at the DEC Enfield facility described in Chapter 8 many aspects of the work were self-contained and required little attention to the work of others; completing other jobs required considerable exchange of information and/or materials. Certain technical tasks (checking quality variances) tended to be solitary activities, while such tasks as scheduling usually involved members of the entire team. The kind of structuring that took place at Enfield shifted the traditional responsibility for work schedules, materials handling, and daily planning from management to the employees. Consequently, the workers had to learn to pay attention to the fact that they were part of a network of other individuals whose work would be affected by their individual decisions. Any failure to honor the interdependencies could result in serious problems for the team.

After diagnosing the nature of the interdependence required, it is important for all members of the team to develop a shared picture of all the interconnections and where they fit in that picture. Sometimes mapping or at least some visual representation of the working relationships among the team members can be useful. This is particularly important in a setting where work demands tend to change and even may be fairly unpredictable. Such conditions often create tension and uncertainty, causing people to focus only on their own jobs without adequate attention to the larger group context. Regular meetings and discussions of task interdependencies can help a team stay on top of changes and stave off their adverse effects.

One of the lessons from Enfield is that the wider the range of employees' knowledge about the overall task and all its aspects, the more effective the team is. It allows for flexibility, job exchanges, workers filling in for one another, and so forth. It also allows employees to negotiate and renegotiate how they spend their time and even when they spend their time. Since the shared goals relate to getting the work done and the responsibility for that lies entirely with the members of the team, it is possible for them to find ways to meet a wide range of needs, including some that are not work-related. One thing we have learned over the years is that employees who are permitted the flexibility to integrate their work and personal lives tend to be more productive and committed than those who are forced to stay within preestablished boundaries. Co-worker commitment can be fostered by encouraging an ongoing process of negotiation among team members around task interdependencies as the situation demands.

One other step that helps to build and maintain effective cooperation is a norms analysis. Every group has norms that pertain to the work and norms that pertain to relationships. It is not atypical for a group to be totally unaware of its norms even though members may feel pressure to conform to them. Even those groups that are aware of their own norms may not take the time to examine them and see if they are still relevant, whether they continue to serve the group well, or whether they have become obsolete or even dysfunctional.

Norms can persist long beyond the time when they helped the team, but as long as no one questions them, they continue to influence behavior. One group I worked with had established an understanding that no member would voice an opinion until the member who had once been their supervisor had expressed his opinion. It was obviously a carryover from the previous hierarchical structure, when it might have been appropriate, but now that it was a self-managing team and the former supervisor was only a team member, it no longer made sense and was, in fact, a constraint. Even after we carried out a norms analysis and the team discussed this particular norm, it took some time and effort to establish a new norm that did not single out the former supervisor as deserving special deference.

It is not always easy to make a group conscious of its work norms. Norms can be deeply embedded in the patterns of work relationships and almost inaccessible to direct discussion. I usually use some experiential technique to bring norms to the surface. One such technique, the Broken Squares Exercise, was described in Chapter 7, but there are a great many available in training and development manuals. Also, it is possible to design and develop a simulation or exercise that is specially suited to a particular team. Although it usually is helpful to have professional expertise (internal or external) available to help design such a process, it is also possible for a team, especially one that is self-managing, to learn to use techniques that facilitate team development. In doing so there are several important factors to keep in mind:

1. Learning best occurs through discovery, which is most likely to take place when people are relaxed and open to new ideas.
2. An effective way to create such an atmosphere is to engage in an activity in which participants do not feel compelled to look good in the eyes of their peers. There

may always be some element of this in any situation, but it can be minimized by keeping the stakes light.

3. Select an exercise or simulation that is far removed from the literal realities of the work. A manufacturing team should use a simulation that is either neutral or places members in a service context. The opposite would hold for a team in a service setting. The principle behind this is that when people are busy paying attention to showing how much they know, they are least open to learning what they do not know.

4. Use an approach that does not fully determine outcomes in advance but permits the emergence of very individual characteristics. There are exercises that are so tightly structured that what will occur is predictable; others more or less set the stage for a wide range of behavior. Time constraints may dictate using the first, but usually the most effective and lasting learning comes from those situations that allow for various outcomes.

5. Make sure that an adequate amount of time is spent in debriefing because that is when the real objectives are achieved. The emphasis should be on identifying the norms that the group carried into the exercise and on the connections between behavior in the exercise and behavior in the team's real operations. It is often tempting for a group to spend an excessive amount of time reliving an exercise, or even criticizing it, and not enough time trying to learn from the experience.

6. Maintain a focus on task interdependence (at least for our purposes here) and do not get caught up in discussing personal style or interpersonal relationships. This is relatively easy to do in the Broken Squares Exercise, but many others tend to encourage discussion of interpersonal dynamics. If the objectives include both areas, attention must be paid to both, but make sure that task issues do not get confused with personal issues.

7. Finally, identify the task norms that need to be established for the team to maximize its effectiveness as a team. It can be useful to list them and even to post them on a wall as a constant reference point and reminder.

The next section looks at the issue of team identity. As we will see, similar exercises can be used to strengthen team identity, but obviously with a different emphasis.

Group Identity and Performance

We know from the research in social psychology and group dynamics that many factors determine the quality of relationships among members of a group and how cohesive that group is likely to be. These factors include similarity in the backgrounds of the members (age, education, race, gender, ethnicity, personal interests), common goals and values, task relatedness, shared successes or failures, a common enemy (boss, competing group), and, most fundamentally, the frequency of interactions among the group members.

We also know that cohesive groups tend to have strong norms for acceptable behavior and attitudes, norms that can be just as powerful as, or even more powerful than, formal rules in influencing employee behavior. In general, groups that are cohesive and have strong norms that bind members to the group also have strong group identities. The group seems to take on a personality of its own, one that is often clearly identifiable from outside and one that differentiates it from any other group. To the members of the group this seems desirable; to others it may not be so desirable, especially if the group tends to close its doors to others, cuts off needed contact with outside groups, withholds important information or resources needed by the system at large, and/or places its own goals above those of the rest of the organization. Furthermore, as pointed out previously, whether such a cohesive group is effective as a team, in the sense that it performs its tasks in the best interests of the organization, depends in part on whether its task norms are congruent with the goals of the organization.

The functional aspect of a cohesive group is that it creates a setting for strong social support and emotional bonding. People by nature are social beings both at work and outside of work; to the extent that employees experience secure membership in a team they feel free to put their energies into mastering and performing their tasks. Groups that lack cohesiveness and, consequently, fail to provide support for their members are not likely to be effective as teams, at least over the long run. Such groups find it difficult to face and deal with conflicts among members, and they do not develop the level of trust that facilitates open exchange of ideas, information, and feelings.

In general, we can say that cohesive groups whose norms are consistent with organizational goals possess the necessary ingredients for becoming effective teams. However, we need to be very careful about how this proposition translates into modern organizations, which are becoming more and more diverse in their employee composition. Instead of similarity in backgrounds, we are finding increasing diversity. In many organizations teams of the future will be composed of people with very different racial and ethnic origins, people with diverse expertise related to complex problems, and, more as the rule than the exception, people whose personal values are very different. The challenge here will be to find ways to build cohesiveness and group identity that offset or override the inherent differences, to find ways to get teams to value their differences and not see them as barriers to effective working relationships.

As changes in the composition of the work force occur, many existing groups will find themselves resisting the change by failing to legitimize new and different individuals as members. Such behavior tends to be damaging to all concerned, even to the group that thinks it is acting in its own best interests. While it is often natural for people to become self-protective when faced with a perceived threat, the persistence of that behavior eventually will become a threat in and of itself. Under these circumstances some kind of intervention is needed, either from management, from an outside consultant, or, ideally, from some member of the group who has the sense and the courage to confront the issue. Since such an action is likely to violate the group's norms, it can feel very risky to a group member. However, very often the member who is willling to take that risk discovers that others are willing to share it.

Since an increasing number of companies are moving to team-based management and are concerned about how to build effective and committed teams, we need to develop new guidelines and concepts for generating cohesiveness in diversity. In the next section I will propose some ways to approach this challenge, but first I want to describe an approach to team building that focuses primarily on team member relationships. This will serve as a basis for managing the problem of cohesiveness when diversity is great.

Team Member Expectations

A group or team is made up of a network of personal relationships. Apart from the various feelings the members have toward one another, including preferred pairings or subgroupings, every member of the group has expectations for her or his own roles and the roles of the others. Usually these expectations pertain to the tasks that have to be performed, but they also might include some of the group maintenance roles, such as making sure all members are listened to, that members feel okay about expressing their ideas or disagreeing with each other, and so forth. When team members fail to live up to the expectations of others, the group as a whole often suffers, especially if reciprocal interdependence is high. This leads to tension and perhaps a deterioration in the group's performance.

Chapter 9 stressed the importance of a manager's willingness to negotiate job expectations with employees as a way to foster commitment. In building a new team or maintaining an ongoing one there are always role expectations to be negotiated and, at some point, renegotiated. (The concept of role renegotiation used here comes from an article written by John Sherwood and John Glidewell in 1972, and from a book by Roger Harrison published in 1976. Complete listings are in the references at the end of the book.) Failure to do this sets the stage for poor performance and bad feelings. Even when two people do not like each other very much, which is not all that infrequent, they still can meet each other's role expectations relative to the task, provided that they understand those expectations and are committed to meeting them. The negotiation process allows for that to happen and may be a step toward better feelings in relationships that can use them. The process of negotiation generates shared ownership of its outcomes, which not only fosters each individual's identification with role(s) to be performed, but also tends to promote stronger co-worker identification insofar as those roles are part of an interdependent network.

There are usually signs that roles require renegotiation. No doubt we have all had times when our own work meant a great deal of pressure to get a job done within some deadline, only to find ourselves pressing too hard and/or working extra hours to meet that commitment. We might succeed, but often we pay a price. When that happens occasionally, it probably does not represent a serious or long-term problem. But when it happens repeatedly, it might call for an examination of self-imposed expectations and/or a renegotiation of some expectations previously negotiated with others.

One might feel some hesitation (out of embarrassment or from some cherished value about living up to one's promises) about going to the boss. Even with peers it probably will be awkward to raise the issue. Whatever the reason, the price we ultimately pay for not initiating a renegotiation can far outweigh the psychological cost of facing the situation directly and at the most opportune time. The situation may even reach a point where the parties affected find it almost impossible to manage the tension that would accompany the process of renegotiation. The result is a seriously damaged working relationship, perhaps even the total dissolution of it. Often some kind of third-party intervention is called for, but equally often no such third party is available.

One may also at times be on the other side of the problem; a co-worker is behaving in ways that reflect some stress or pressure and, therefore, one needs to initiate a conversation leading to a redefinition of expectations. In fact, a manager's willingness to do that can free others to do the same and can establish a norm of reciprocity around rescuing team members when the signals are there. One might even be the third party who can intervene in a situation involving employees or colleagues who need to renegotiate mutual expectations. It can be well worth one's while to learn more about the process and to develop the requisite skills to manage it.

There are several very simple rules of thumb relative to role negotiation. They hark back to some of the most basic principles we all learned about effective interpersonal relations, but they are worth restating here. Besides, even under the best of circumstances we can easily forget the basics, and when it comes to the need to renegotiate role expectations, we are not talking about the best of circumstances. The rules are:

1. First, ask what assumptions one is making about one's role in the task and in relation to others involved in that task. Also examine the basis or source of those expectations and whether some reality testing is needed. Often we fall into the trap of operating on old assumptions, even when circumstances and/or people have changed. Chances are that some changed realities are demanding revised expectations and they need to be discussed.

2. Check the assumptions with relevant others. Even if the assumptions turn out to have been correct in the first place, the act of checking them opens the door for others to do the same. However, the likely result is that some revisions in thinking are called for on the part of both or all parties. Often, people express relief and appreciation that someone was willing to take the initiative because others were sitting on some tension about meeting their own, often untested, role assumptions.

3. Carefully map the job interconnections so that everyone has a clear picture, especially of exactly how each person's role affects others'. It also will make clear just how any failure to meet role expectations can affect others and the whole team effort, sometimes even the system at large. The mapping also serves another function. It provides some shared boundaries and structure that help reduce tension, build confidence, and strengthen team member bonds. Failure to reduce member tension tends to result in driving individuals back into their own narrow frames of reference, usually in the misguided service of self-protection.

4. The final step is for each individual to make sure that there are no conflicting expectations. This is a notorious problem in matrix organizations in which a person might have more than one boss. It can be a bit complicated to sort out the conflicting expectations and strike some kind of balance. However, failure to do so can result in further deterioration in performance. It is important that the resolution of the conflicts involve all those concerned in order to provide an opportunity to establish common understanding about everyone's role and to avoid diverse interpretations of each individual's expected behavior.

A useful additional step, which comes from Harrison's book (1976), involves having individuals articulate what behaviors they would like to see others stop (or decrease), start (or increase) and continue. This is often best done in writing, followed by a discussion, in pairs, of what each is asking of the other. When conducted properly, which usually means with the full consent of all parties, the process is helpful in building better understanding between co-workers and among the members of the team as a whole. Since the focus is on behavior, the process tends to avoid attributions and interpretations. (For a more complete, yet concise description of the application of this approach, see Chapter 13 of Thomas Gilmore's 1988 book, *Making a Leadership Change.)*

The only other thing I would suggest is that the team members discuss their perceptions and feelings about role negotiation, what its costs and benefits are, and how it might be improved. Someone usually suggests that it be conducted more frequently in order to avoid a buildup of the kind of tension that pushes people into avoidance and only makes things worse. For the sake of group cohesiveness and mutual commitment, the process works best not as a technique, but as an ongoing way of life.

Joseph Heller, in his novel *Something Happened* (1985), provides a wonderful example of a setting in which untested assumptions and a failure to renegotiate mutual expectations result in a situation bordering on the bizarre.

In the office in which I work there are five people of whom I am afraid. Each of these five is afraid of four people (excluding overlaps), for a total of twenty, and each of these twenty people is afraid of six people, making a total of one hundred and twenty people who are feared by at least one person. Each of these one hundred and twenty people is afraid of the other one hundred and nineteen, and all of these one hundred and forty-five people are afraid of the twelve men at top who helped found and build the company and now own and direct it (p. 9).

Are these people living in a less than ideal organizational climate? Absurd as it may sound, when I read this description to managers I often see heads nodding in recognition. It is not exactly what I would label a high commitment system.

Negotiation and Diversity

It is one thing for co-workers to negotiate mutual expectations when they come from similar backgrounds and share a common cultural perspective. The all-white, thirty-year-old male Anglo-Saxon group, apart from personality differences, usually finds it easier to develop mutually agreed-upon expectations than a group that is more mixed in gender, race, age, or nationality. Individuals carry with them certain ingrained expectations for themselves, which are reflections of their upbringing and the cultural values with which they were imbued. The potential for misunderstandings and misguided role expectations can be enormous. But this is one of the challenges of today's organizations, which are becoming more culturally diverse and, it is hoped, more balanced with respect to gender and race.

The past decade has seen a proliferation of books, articles, training programs, and other organizational efforts to make people more conscious of differences, to value those differences, and to deliberately seek to capitalize on them in building a strong work force. Although not all organizations have the same level of need for diversity in terms of mission or market, most eventually will be faced with the fact that the composition of our work force is changing dramatically. What is now the white majority may not be that in the future. While I cannot go into a detailed discussion of all the ways in which managers might learn to deal with diversity, since that is not my area of expertise and would certainly deserve greater attention than I can give it here, I do want to offer some guidelines for using role negotiation, as described in the previous section, when the composition of the group or team is highly diverse.

Metaphors as Conceptual Bridges. Let me relate an example of a work group situation in which one member behaved in ways that were disruptive and counterproductive. He happened to be a native of Venezuela who was educated in the United States. He was an engineer, very bright, and eager to prove himself to the team to which he was assigned. I was present as a process consultant, mainly for the period of project planning and design. There were eight members on the team, mostly engineers, a theoretical physicist, and a financial manager. The group was all male and the only non-American was Juan, the Venezuelan.

After several meetings it was evident that the group had a problem. Juan contributed his ideas only when asked by Ed, the senior engineer. He never offered opinions on his own and always looked to Ed before responding to questions from anyone else. Since his specialty was critical to the project, Juan's behavior only bogged things down and annoyed everyone. Even after being asked to change his behavior, the pattern persisted.

At one point during a lunch break I was speaking with Juan about his country and its customs when it struck me that he sounded different than he did in the team sessions. He was more animated and spontaneous, and he seemed to relate quite freely with me. I pointed this out, which made him somewhat uncomfortable, but he replied by explaining how different it feels to be in a group that is not "family." He went on to explain that where he grew up, most people worked in companies that were family owned and many people in the same work setting were relatives. It was obvious that family was very important to Juan and, in fact, was his personal metaphor for organizational life.

I asked him to imagine that the team members were family members and to tell me who each individual would be in his family. He described Ed as the father and the rest of the team as either brothers or cousins, depending upon how close he felt to them. He said I was a brother, but I did not know whether he was trying to be kind to me. I asked Juan why he seemed to refuse to take initiative and why he did not feel free to respond to his "brothers'" questions. He said that in his country it is important to know your place in the family and always to show respect for the father. We talked more about how difficult it must be for him to change his ways, but that for the sake of the project and due to the need for his free participation, it was important that he attempt to make the changes.

When the team went back to work I shared with the members the conversation between Juan and me (with Juan's permission). It opened up a useful discussion about the different metaphors we carry with us and how easy it is for misunderstandings to occur when people assume that others are thinking in terms of their own working metaphors. The members actually took some time to share their metaphors related to work, organization, and the role of a manager. I will skip the details, but I can report that it was a very enlightening experience, and it gave me a way to conceptualize personal and cultural differences.

Although we may not always be conscious of them, each of us carries around images and metaphors about life, work, ourselves, our families, friends, and the organizations for which we work. Many metaphors are common to or shared by people with similar backgrounds, and many are more typical of one culture than of another. Juan's family metaphor was probably more typical of a Latin country than a northern European country. Sports metaphors are very familiar to Americans, while nature metaphors are characteristic of Far Eastern countries.

My point here is that the use of metaphors can be at least one key to bridging the gap between cultures or, for that matter, between any groups or individuals whose backgrounds are fundamentally different. When people share their metaphors they are sharing their images of the world and their places in it. It can have a very powerful effect on the level of mutual understanding among individuals and on their level of appreciation for each other. Once understood, Juan behaved differently, but he never let go of his family metaphor. Similarly, the other members of the team learned to react to Juan differently, now that they understood him better, but they did not change their demands on his talents. In fact, they came to appreciate those talents even more.

Many approaches to managing cultural diversity tend to emphasize differences in language, customs, and values. However, the most successful also focus on the fundamental thought processes, especially the underlying structure of thought that differentiates one culture from another. Metaphors are useful representations of those thought processes and can serve as powerful tools for building the bridges necessary for a culturally diverse team to work effectively. What may appear to be a serious disagreement between members can turn out to be related to differences in the way each translates the content of an issue into his or her own image about what is happening.

In *Images of Organizations* (1986), Gareth Morgan offers a range of metaphors that can be applied to organizational life. If one individual interprets a problem through a machine metaphor, for example, and the other interprets that same problem using the metaphor of a living organism or a human brain, each will develop a different understanding of that problem and a different approach to its solution. Both positions might be reasonable and valid, but neither individual is likely to see the validity of the other's position unless they can share each other's metaphors and explore ways to build a common approach.

It is not easy to get people into each other's frames of reference, and I do not suggest any formula or procedure for building metaphor bridges. However, it seems that the most useful way to begin is by having members of a highly diverse team, especially where some strong cultural differences exist, share their different working metaphors. This can be done through words, but often visual images provide even more effective ways to communicate. They serve as a visual representation of a metaphor. Since part of the objective is to build co-worker commitment, it is valuable for the team to determine how it should go about the activity. Coming in with a predetermined design or a package off the shelf is to some extent a contradiction of the objective. Even if the group creates a procedure that is less than elegant, it can serve its purpose better than one that is not owned by the group.

Returning to the case of Juan for a moment, there was one very interesting exchange between Juan and Ed that illustrated the impact of the metaphor analysis the group did. During one of the meetings Juan was presenting some technical analysis of a difficult problem. It was clear that he knew more about it than anyone there, had done his homework, and was well prepared. When he was finished he stood there waiting for something; no one knew what. I asked him what was going on and he replied that he was somehow hoping to hear some special praise from Ed, who happened to be the least qualified person in the group to judge Juan's presentation. Then Juan smiled and said that he still had not let go of Ed as his "father" and still needed that sense of personal confirmation from him. Ed said, "You were just wonderful, Juan." Everyone burst out laughing, including Juan.

As a final point, I would suggest that the steps in role negotiation, when combined with an exploration of group members' metaphors, can be effective for team building in a multicultural context. It is also important to recognize that even in groups that are fairly homogeneous, there is still likely to be some diversity in the ways that members see the world. An analysis of members' metaphors can be beneficial and is usually intrinsically interesting to everyone.

Team-Centered Performance Appraisal

Chapter 6 offered some guidelines for building a performance appraisal system that is commitment oriented. The final section of this chapter focuses on specific aspects of performance appraisal that are related to groups or teams. The approach I suggest recognizes that there is a variety of roles and functions that team members serve and that they are related to both the task of the group and maintenance of the group. (This concept comes from a 1948 article entitled "Functional Roles of Group Members" by Benne and Sheats. For the complete reference, see the reference list at the end of the book.) I have seen only one performance evaluation procedure that gives equal weight to both. It is used by a medium-sized manufacturing plant in New Hampshire. Its designer took a truly team-centered approach to evaluation, giving equal weight to contributions to both task and maintenance.

Task Functions. The task functions, or roles, usually served by members of the group include:

1. Initiating ideas
2. Seeking information and opinions
3. Giving information and opinions
4. Clarifying problems
5. Summarizing discussions
6. Testing for consensus

Very often a status system develops for these various roles, which may or may not work for the group. For example, it is not unusual for the member who has the most information to be given the greatest degree of influence, even past the point where information is the central issue. Because tasks usually have several stages, the different functions tend to vary in importance in relation to the given stage of the process. Therefore, when it comes to the evaluation of a member's contribution to the group's task, it is important for the group to have documented each member's role over time. Eventually, most members of a team become skilled in a variety of functions, and no one member will be identified exclusively as the "idea generator" or the "summarizer" or whatever.

Maintenance Functions. The maintenance roles, sometimes called social roles, include:

1. Gate keeping (facilitating participation and communication)
2. Expressing and encouraging others to express feelings
3. Helping to harmonize tensions
4. Facilitating compromise
5. Helping to monitor standards and goals
6. Supporting others

These functions, while not as directly and clearly related to team performance, are just as vital as the task functions. However, they rarely are recognized for their value, although many programs designed to train managers as team leaders include these roles as part of what they learn. When it comes to evaluating a member's contribution to the team, most of the weight is given to task-related functions.

The Need for a Balanced Approach. For a performance appraisal system to actually help build co-worker commitment it needs to be based on principles that do not generate competition or even comparison. The assumption must be made and honored that every member can serve a valuable role and that it is the job of the team as a whole to create opportunities for its members to learn and develop a range of skills related to both the task and maintenance functions of the group.

Furthermore, it is important to recognize that every team has its own personality and needs to have flexibility, within some general organizational boundaries, in managing the appraisal process, despite the organization's desire for common appraisal standards and procedures.

A failure on the part of a team member to contribute in some way should be considered unacceptable, but an effective team accepts and encourages a diversity of roles for members to play, depending upon their strengths and preferences, and encourages members to constantly work to improve their performance of those roles and to learn new ones.

The Enfield plant of DEC used a knowledge-based approach to employee pay. What I am suggesting is also a knowledge-based approach, but one that includes the application of knowledge about group process. The criteria for this approach can best be developed by the organization through team representation, but the application of those criteria are best left to each team. Self-managing teams need to be self-evaluating teams. Anything short of that is a mixed message, at best.

A Final Message about Teams

Working in a team that is performing well and in which the members are supportive is an enjoyable and rewarding experience. But never forget that the team is only one link in a larger network of teams, all hopefully contributing to the same purposes. Tom Isgar, in an excellent manager's guide to building teamwork, *The Ten Minute Team* (1989), offers the following guidelines:

- Teams must be clear on how they support organizational purposes.
- Purpose provides daily guidance as well as future goals.
- Individuals should be able to see the link between their work, their team's purpose, and the organization's purpose.
- Teams need to refocus on purpose from time to time (p. 21).

Chapter 11 focuses on building commitment at the system level by fostering organizational identification. When strong team performance is combined with strong organizational identification, we have all the potential for creating a high performance system, which should be the ultimate goal of any organization today.

Building a High Commitment System

A manager at a manufacturing facility dedicated to building system-wide teamwork stated, "If we could create an atmosphere of teamwork in the whole organization, we wouldn't have a problem in getting the teams to work well." His statement reflected the fact that simply focusing on team building is not enough to sustain teamwork over the long run; it also depends upon an atmosphere of teamwork company-wide. In fact, it is relatively easy to maintain a local focus where the outcomes and benefits of teamwork are tangible and visible. Building and maintaining teamwork in the larger system is much more difficult because the benefits are less tangible and may not be forthcoming until some time in the future.

Furthermore, as part of a management team, one tends to identify most strongly with peers or colleagues who share the same immediate objectives. Support for and commitment to each other in a management team can be a sustaining and driving force in the success of the organization, but sometimes it takes a strong, conscious effort by members to pull their perspectives away from the team and into the larger organization.

This chapter looks at the various obstacles to building a high commitment system and ways to overcome them. As reflected in the research data, one central issue appears to be related to cooperation at a system level. The previous chapter examined this issue as it relates to co-worker commitment; now we consider its significance in the context of relationships among groups in the organization.

System-wide Interdependence

It is important to keep in mind that the effects of a lack of attention to interdependence relates directly to the type of interdependence required. Departments that are essentially autonomous and whose decisions have little effect on other departments can afford to be less aware of the relationships. This is pooled interdependence. In cases of either serial or reciprocal interdependence, commitment to the organization becomes critical and can make a major difference in the success of the enterprise.

In most cases an organization nowadays operates with a mixture of the three types, especially the second two. In an interview, a high level engineer at an aerospace company described to me some of the problems that were occurring in what he identified as the "hand-off" process in the company. Design engineers would send their specifications on to manufacturing engineers, only to have them returned with complaints that they were not realistic. Then the design engineers would complain that manufacturing did not know what they were talking about because the designs were perfectly clear and realistic. Back and forth it went until someone got the bright idea to set up a task force made up of both design and manufacturing engineers to work together right from the beginning.

What had been happening was that the design and manufacturing stages, which do occur serially, involved information exchange that needed to occur reciprocally. Until the reciprocal exchange occurred the problem could not be resolved. This is not atypical of what goes on in all kinds of organizations today. The operational aspects of the work may be sequential, but the information exchanges necessary for effective decision-making are reciprocal. In short, it is a mixed picture with more than one type of interdependence needed at the same time. Attention to this factor is essential to building a high commitment system, but there are a number of others that are equally important.

Managing Boundaries among Groups

The barriers that often exist among groups (departments, usually) in an organization are direct reflections of the barriers that exist among the managers or leaders of those groups. However, there is a chicken-and-egg problem here: Did the barriers among the managers occur because of inherent differences that exist among their respective groups? Or did the interpersonal conflicts that exist among the managers get translated into intergroup conflicts? In most cases it is a little of both.

The important issue may not be a precise diagnosis of the causes, but more the question of ways to reduce or even eliminate the walls. The responsibility of the manager is to build commitments to peers that cut across any inherent differences in professions. Such commitments set a tone or climate of shared purpose that goes beyond parochial concerns.

The Loyalty Bind. Such efforts are not easy. One of the hardest issues to get past is the "loyalty bind." A member who no longer subscribes to the group's stereotype of the so-called enemy—usually because direct experience has disconfirmed that stereotype—is likely to be seen as a traitor. ("Whose side are you on, anyway?" is a familiar cry.) However, if that person pushes the group into the same kind of direct contact with the alleged enemy, they too will see the stereotypes dissolve. And the process will be reciprocal.

The bonds that develop from interpersonal commitment among peers are powerful and can serve the organization well—provided that they serve as a springboard for building commitments *across* the boundaries of the groups and not as barriers that generate competition and conflict. Although people naturally gravitate to those with similar interests, goals, and beliefs, they also can find it rewarding and enriching to interact with those who are different. However, the organization must encourage, support, require, and reward the effort because insularity tends to emerge more easily.

The Manager in the Middle. The well-known manager in the middle often finds that it is impossible to satisfy the demands of the boss and the needs of subordinates at the same time. For example, a manager may be trying to get as much of the financial pie as possible for her own department, only to find that pressures from peers (other department heads) pull her in the opposing direction. Even perceiving the legitimacy of others' needs can be experienced as disloyalty to her own constituents, only to be reinforced when she tries to explain a shift in position to those who were counting on her in the first place.

There often are times when a commitment to someone who has served the company loyally for years is no longer in the best interests of the organization. One example that comes to mind is a case in which the head of a legal department retained the services of his office manager despite that individual's very disruptive, interfering behavior. The endless complaints from staff members, many of whom eventually left the firm, failed to shake the department head's resolve to keep the manager in his position. Emotionally, the department head was strongly committed to the office manager and was placing that commitment above commitment to the firm. Such behavior is understandable, even to be admired in some sense, but clearly was based upon a set of priorities that were inadequately related to the interests of the organization.

A frequent example of this kind of dilemma occurs when a company is cutting certain functions, perhaps eliminating whole departments, and is, at the same time, trying to salvage as many people as possible by shifting them into job openings that may be less suitable for their talents. The effects can be disastrous for the individuals being moved and for those who depend upon competence and experience in the jobs affected. There may be a humanistic intent behind such moves, but the net effect all too often is humiliation for those moved and a real loss of job commitment on the part of others.

Maintaining Organizational Priorities. The way to prevent such difficulties is to establish and communicate a clear set of priorities with respect to the goals and values of the organization. With each employee it is important to keep those priorities at the forefront of job expectations so that there is less chance of misunderstanding later on.

Most employees can learn to understand and accept the priorities of an organization, and they do not necessarily feel that commitments are being violated when layoffs occur in times of hardship. One small manufacturing firm in New England recently had to let go of twenty percent of its labor force. As a company with a history of commitment to the welfare of its employees and that seemed to elicit strong commitment in return, the situation represented a real crisis. The company had always held to a principle of seniority, which today is becoming more and more obsolete, and chose to maintain that principle in the crisis. It was a clear criterion and generally accepted by all employees. Painful as it was, there was almost no griping or bitterness from those who had to leave, only a general sadness for having to separate from the work and people they had come to value.

As long as there is a goal, a purpose, a problem, or a principle that provides a focus over and above the special interests of two or more parties, the trap of a loyalty bind can be avoided. One party need not be forced to pay the price for the demands of the other. Even when the situation looks like a zero-sum game, shifting to a problem-centered way of thinking usually reveals ways to honor commitments that at first seem inherently contradictory.

Managing the Inherent Conflicts. We talk about inherent conflicts in organizations: marketing goals versus quality control; sophisticated engineering versus simple manufacturing methods; quality patient care versus rapid turnover of available beds; quality teaching versus the efficiency of large classes. In many cases it may be necessary to compromise and make trade-offs; but in many instances it is possible to be creative and to maintain a commitment to goals that otherwise pull people in opposite directions. The use of quality circles resulted (where done appropriately) in both better quality products and greater efficiency in production. The creation of medical teams improved patient care and, in fact, helped patients to get well faster. The technology of group methods in the classroom provided opportunities for students to work with and learn from each other even in very large classes.

It is natural for different segments of an organization to see things from their own narrow perspectives. The boundaries tend to become hardened and difficult to overcome. The result is that even if managers can elicit very strong commitment to the different goals of the different groups, they might be faced with the problem of trying to extend that commitment beyond those boundaries so that everyone is working toward some common goals. Many managers are not successful at doing that because they tend to identify with one or another group and see themselves as part of a status system, a pecking order, and they put their own interests as high in the order as possible. If a company is engineering driven and a manager is an engineer, the natural tendency will be to keep engineering interests at the forefront of the company's policies. Then, the commitment will tend to be to other engineers, to engineering work itself, and to an organization whose mission and identity reflect engineering values.

The result is that one may get a high level of commitment from engineers, but one also may find less than adequate commitment from other segments of the company. In effect, one does not have an integrated system in which all the various separate goals link together to form an overarching common purpose with which everyone can identify.

Conflicting Commitments in Complex Structures

At one time a person's work identity was simple and predictable. A salesperson identified with the sales function and with the people in that function; the same principle held for people in manufacturing. Similarly for organizations organized by product line, sales identification, and therefore the sales people's commitment, was directly related to that line.

In many of today's organizations, where matrix structures are common, managers may find themselves simultaneously pulled in more than one direction. Do they identify more strongly with their functional areas (professions) or with the product line they are serving? Can they be equally committed to both? In successful matrix structures the commitment is to the overall mission or purpose of the organization; it overrides any more local commitments. In this sense one can identify with more than one group or boss.

However, this does not occur automatically; in fact, to generate commitment to an overarching goal, those who manage at the top must make that goal visible and relevant to all levels. A failure to do so will produce the most undesirable effect, namely commitment to oneself. In short, the ambiguity created by multiple bosses and multiple group memberships in a complex organization is likely, in the absence of a clear overall goal, to result in self-serving behavior. In such a case the individuals might be highly committed to their jobs, but only to the jobs, and not to co-workers or the organization.

Whether one manages in a traditionally structured organization or one that is more complex, and probably more inherently confusing, there are a number of ways to maximize employee commitment to the overall work effort as opposed to narrower sets of goals. Some methods to try include the following:

1. Structure the work so that accomplishing goals requires resources that cut across the natural boundaries associated with the usual departmental or professional interests. Companies that are organized around functional areas (as opposed to product or service lines) tend to have more problems with commitment to company goals (as opposed to departmental goals).

2. Where it is not possible to restructure, create planning groups and problem-solving groups with heterogeneous membership. Require that they meet regularly and frequently. Also, whenever possible, rotate membership in the groups. This approach serves to keep people aware of broad interests and views, rather than parochial concerns.

3. Orient new members of the organization to all facets of its operations, even if their jobs require a more limited perspective. In the long run, as they gain experience and move up in the system, they will need to broaden their views and knowledge anyway. If the process starts early enough it plants the seeds for a more integrated view of the organization than if parochialism is allowed to solidify.

4. Where possible build career tracks that allow, and even encourage, movement across traditional departmental or professional lines. If an engineer wishes to change careers at age forty, it might be possible to transfer his or her talents into a new career within the company and not lose a valuable resource. Some of the best marketing or sales people were once the most creative engineers or research people. Building the options into the total system fosters commitment to that total system. This may be especially important if the organization is in a period of transition.

Organizations in Transition

An increasing number of companies today, especially the small and the medium-sized high tech ones, are struggling with the transition from entre-preneur-founder domination to an enterprise more formally structured and professionally managed. The kind of shared vision and collective commit-ment that holds a company together in its formative years can easily get lost in a proliferation of new people, new procedures, and complexities of communications.

Unfortunately, many companies attempt to make the transition by hiring managers more appropriately trained to manage larger, more established systems. The new managers lack the experience and knowledge that would enable them to keep alive the spirit of the founder's vision. They do not even appreciate the emergent cultural fabric that historically held people together during the years of struggle and growth. It is the loss of historical roots, accompanied by the sheer increase in numbers of people who never get touched by the founder's vision, that eventually erodes the kind of employee commitment that made the organization successful in the first place.

Many organizations today, especially those built on a tradition of stability and a reputation for high standards of service to people (insurance companies and banks), are feeling the pressure to change, to modernize their methods of operation, to computerize. Furthermore, they are discovering that much of what motivated their employees in the past, the former bases of commit-ment, no longer seem relevant to the young people entering their organiza-tions. I hear managers complain that commitment to a profession or to one's own career seems to be more prevalent than commitment to the setting, its mission, or its people.

While it may seem logical and tempting to try to overcome professional loyalty by trying to engender organizational loyalty, a manager would, in fact, be better off actually supporting the commitment of employees to their professions. This helps to build an association between professional goals and organizational rewards, the net result being commitment to both. One way to do this is to encourage, support, and even require contact across professional lines, but at the same time build on the employee's own professional expertise as the basis for those contacts. The individual is thereby rewarded for both professional and organizational commitment.

In addition to those steps already suggested to minimize group barriers and keep people focused on organizational priorities, I suggest three additional, straightforward, though not always easy, procedures:

1. Create substructures that foster employee contacts with each other and that allow some autonomy in task design and management.
2. Create teams of managers that cut across the substructures and give them the job of keeping the system integrated.
3. Meet frequently with these management teams to get their insights on problems, but, even more important, to share the leader's continuing aspirations and goals for the organization.

These suggestions, which are an extension of the four offered earlier, are built on the premise that the company has hired reasonably competent managers who share its vision (or at least are in the process of internalizing it), whose own goals are congruent with those of the company, and who are willing to commit their support and cooperation to each other.

Some executives, especially those who simply cannot bear to let go of their "child," spend time walking around the company. That can be fine, since it often conveys a genuine interest in everyone's welfare, and it may even be an indirect way of sharing a vision. But it can cut both ways; it can make employees nervous or suspicious and might actually result in lower commitment than would otherwise be the case. A wise manager is careful to gather data on the impact of "walking around" and then make an intelligent choice for the future. Employees who have been around for many years may understand the intent; others may attribute the wrong intent to that behavior.

Fostering Commitment through Manageable Units

We know that in very large organizations it is difficult to maintain an overall sense of common purpose and some degree of cohesiveness. Many companies are experimenting with the use of new structures, like the strategic business unit, as a means of creating more manageable enterprises. W. L. Gore, Inc., tries not to allow any given plant to grow beyond two hundred employees. Raritan River Corp. is a small steel mill that has combined state-of-the-art technology with effective management practices to create a profitable company in an otherwise dying industry. Why is Raritan so successful while major steel companies are going deeper into the red? It developed a system that is manageable in size and that allows its managers to make decisions and take initiative, thereby fostering a firm sense of identification with the company, the work effort, and the people in the organization.

The concepts of cost center, profit center, and strategic business unit are attempts to create boundaries or territories that generate a sense of involvement. That sense of involvement can permeate the total unit from top to bottom precisely because the unit is the whole within which every member can relate the parts. But, size limitation alone cannot do the job of generating commitment. The management philosophy and practices that small size can accommodate must also be in place.

The Importance of Vision and Empowerment. Although the importance of visionary leadership was discussed at some length in Chapter 3, the issue is worth some additional emphasis in relation to the problem of size. The processes of sharing a vision and empowering people certainly are more readily carried out in smaller units. But, most corporations do not have much choice about their size; they are simply too large to embrace. How can the processes of the smaller firm be transferred to the larger ones?

Organizations that are bound by the rules and constraints of a bureaucratic structure often fail to foster the open channels needed for vision sharing. A notion suggested to me by James Clawson at the Darden School of the University of Virginia provides an interesting way to think about the problem. He suggested the concept of *visiocracy,* a Latin/Greek term meaning 'rule of vision.' Such an organization is structured around the attainment of the overall vision. People are measured by their progress in helping to achieve the vision, usually are members of the organization because their personal aspirations match the organization's vision, and are constantly organizing and reorganizing work in ways that help accomplish the vision.

Balancing Formal and Informal Systems

In many respects managing the system overall is an attempt to strike a balance between what people are inclined to do naturally without any rules and what must be required of them in a more formal way in order to ensure a coordinated effort. In this regard I want to suggest an approach that focuses on the physical architecture of the work environment as a key element in building a high commitment system.

The Impact of Architecture. A number of years ago I attended a conference of architects, graphic designers, and social scientists held in Aspen, Colorado. The conference was about the relationship between architectural forms and the purposes they serve. There were two sharply contrasting schools of thought represented: one school emphasized form for its own sake, insisting that the purity of artistic integrity should be maintained irrespective of the functions or activities that go on within those forms; the other school viewed form as serving function, stressing that human beings have to live and move about inside whatever structures the architect creates. From the point of view of the latter school, the role of the architect is to create forms that are not only attractive artistically, but also serve the needs of the people using them.

It struck me then, and on many occasions since, that organizational forms often completely ignore what is supposed to go on within them, that they even at times seem to create every obstacle imaginable to the very processes that they presumably were intended to serve. That is precisely why we have alternative organizational forms and always may be faced with the task of modifying them as the purposes they serve change.

Shortly after attending that conference I was asked to give a talk to a group of organizational consultants on the subject of the Aspen conference. As it turned out, the room we met in was completely wrong for my purposes. I took advantage of the opportunity by having the group focus on our immediate physical setting, what purposes it might best serve, and then look at the kind of setting that would serve our own purposes better. That led very naturally into a discussion of the relationship between form and purpose in the context of organizational design and development.

I also have noticed what seems to happen on college or university campuses when pathways are paved for students to use. If the pathways do not provide the most direct route from point to point, they tend to be ignored. The students, and I imagine many faculty, simply cross the lawns, usually on a direct line to their point of destination. Then the administration tries to control this behavior with signs or ropes or other objects to discourage walking on the grass, only to find them ignored. I remember distinctly the time my own university, in a fit of absolute resignation, finally began to pave the most worn out grassy areas that obviously were serving as natural paths. In effect, the informal, natural behavior of people provided the guidelines for the more formal boundaries within which they were to operate. It may be a bit like calling a break in a meeting after noticing that a third of the group already has started out of the room, but at least it recognizes certain human realities.

The work of Fritz Steele (1973) probably represents one of the most highly developed and successful approaches to the design of physical environments in organizations. At the heart of Steele's approach is a philosophy that physical settings or arrangements that are congruent with both the required work patterns and the natural social patterns of employees work best to facilitate productive behavior. Furthermore, to the extent that these arrangements foster employee interactions they also build positive working relationships.

Most organizations design their physical settings to conserve space, to accommodate equipment, to isolate executives, to symbolize status, and to serve a myriad of purposes that may have very little to do with getting the job done. Engineers are grouped together, administrative services are housed in a single area even though they may serve many groups throughout the organization, accounting people tend to be closeted somewhere out of the way, and designers are grouped together to share expensive equipment.

All these arrangements may make perfect sense from certain points of view, or they would not occur. However, as organizations find themselves serving many different markets or customers in ways that require more integration of the specialties, the physical arrangements become impediments that need to be changed. Earlier we looked at ways to overcome barriers by using lateral structures, task forces, and liaison people, but not ways that necessarily involve moving people around and changing their physical locations. Yet this may be the most direct and powerful approach to the problem. Let us look at an example.

The Steelcase Corporate Development Center. Steele was one of the principal consultants to Steelcase when it built its new Corporate Development Center (CDC) in Grand Rapids, Michigan, in 1989. The overriding objective was to create a setting that would foster a total sense of integration among the employees, a high level of awareness of the overall organization and a commitment to its mission, and a maximum flow of information throughout the system. The designers took into account not only the behavior and interactions required to do the work, but also the personal and social needs that employees brought to the situation.

Instead of establishing a home base for every employee in his or her own discipline (engineers all together, marketing people all in the same area, and financial functions grouped together), employees were organized into integrated "neighborhoods," where people from the various professions would interact daily and have continually high visibility to one another. There would be few opportunities for misconceptions and stereotypes to develop because daily contacts would encourage employees to know each other as individuals rather than as members of this group or that group. The different disciplines, therefore, would come to understand each others' worlds and to appreciate their mutual effect on one another, especially where serial or reciprocal interdependence was important.

In addition, recognizing that employees often needed relatively isolated areas to work on projects without interruption or distraction, meeting rooms and offices were provided for projects and were, in effect, owned by the project teams for the life of that particular work. This practice allowed teams to leave their charts and equipment in the work spaces without having to pack up every time they ended a work session. But the employees always returned to their home bases for messages and routine work and also to stay connected with important issues and events that were organization-wide.

Another interesting feature of Steelcase CDC is the overall design of the building. It is a four-sided pyramid with a central atrium within which is a series of escalators that provide riders with a total view of the company. It is possible to see most of the comings and goings, as well as the working activities in the neighborhoods. There are attractive break areas, both indoors and outdoors, on the various levels of the pyramid where employees can gather for coffee and general conversation. These areas are among the most attractive in the building, so that people actually are encouraged to use them. Evidently, Steelcase has little concern about employees wasting their time in idle conversation. The overall openness of the physical environment also conveys the company's values about openness in general, what Steele describes as a "high disclosure" setting.

The Steelcase example represents a true integration of the formal and informal organization. Most important, however, it emphasizes the informal as the foundation of its operation, whereas most organizations begin with the formal and accept the informal as a necessary phenomenon. To quote from an internal document at Steelcase, "Interaction that stimulates and enhances creative work is almost always informal, often resulting from chance encounters, perhaps in the hallway, perhaps at a pot of coffee."

Many organizations could take a cue from Steelecase and could institute major improvements in employees' commitment system-wide if they were to pay more attention to the physical setting within which their employees work. Simple and often painfully obvious rearrangements can produce significant changes for the better. It is very difficult for individuals to ignore each other for long when they are sitting near each other and/or constantly passing each other in the corridors or in the break areas. If the individuals are from different backgrounds, eventually the differences will rub off and lead to mutual understanding and to developing common objectives in the best interest of the company as a whole. Members of the same profession talk about common professional interests; members of different professions, but from the same company, talk about common company issues. It is natural and informal, but it clearly reinforces the required and formal aspects of the organization.

An Overview

In a recent article, Weckler and Lawrence (1991) discuss the recruitment and selection processes that are likely to create a high commitment organization. In that article they list the key elements of the kind of organizational culture their approach is designed for. These elements seem to capture, from a slightly different perspective, the essential qualities emphasized in this chapter. Their list includes:

- A management philosophy of mutual trust and respect
- Strong leadership with a clear vision of what the organization can be
- High levels of employee participation in decision-making
- Organization of employees into teams

- Broad job descriptions
- Compensation based on employees' skill level and performance
- Flat organizational structures that are often business-unit based
- Management that projects a strong commitment to quality and continuous improvement (p. 38)

Adherence to these principles can go a long way toward developing a high commitment organization, but there remain a number of difficult problems for managers to overcome in their efforts to create such a setting. The final chapter of the book examines some of them.

Chapter 12

Some Current Issues
for Managers

This chapter covers a number of issues with which organizations are struggling. I have chosen to address those I have found through direct experience, or through the experiences of many of my professional colleagues, to be most salient to managerial practices today. There is no particular order to the topics covered, so it is possible to skip around or go directly to those of particular interest. The topics include:

- Finding committed people
- Dealing with times of retrenchment
- Commitment and financial control
- Managing conflicting commitments
- The uses of physical space
- The importance of rituals and ceremonies
- Sustaining commitment in periods of crisis
- Balancing work and personal life
- Teaching about commitment

Finding Committed People

Many organizations today face a basic dilemma in recruiting and hiring when it comes to finding committed employees. I hear managers complain that they can find people who identify with their work and their own careers, but show little inclination to commit to the goals of the organization or the people in it. However, there is rarely any reason for a new recruit to identify with a setting with which he or she has had no history. That's a process that takes time and depends upon the kinds of opportunities the organization provides to draw the individual into a lasting relationship.

Managers are probably dealing with roughly three categories of people: (1) those who are naturally inclined for whatever reasons to seek a "home" in an organization and will, consequently, tend to internalize the goals of the system and develop close relationships with its members; (2) those whose focus of commitment is strongly related to their work and profession, but who, as a result of rewarding experiences in a given setting, broaden their commitment to encompass other people (boss, colleagues, subordinates) and the organization's mission; and (3) those who are so strongly identified with their work that they never bother to look around in order to connect with their surroundings. The last group may tend to be self-serving (consciously or unconsciously) or, at best, indifferent to others; many may look at the organization only as a place where they can "do their thing," ready to jump to whatever setting will best serve that end.

Successful recruiting draws in people from the first two categories and screens out those in the third, unless they are needed for temporary assignments or projects, in which case job commitment is the most relevant factor. Whatever recruiting needs managers have, however, they still want to be in a position to make intelligent choices about whom to hire, what can be expected from new hires, and what managers need to provide for them. When trying to build a solid foundation for future growth, too many from category three, for example, can be detrimental. On the other hand, there is always a risk that employees who need a home badly will allow identification with others to overshadow commitment to professional development.

I suspect that the middle category is the largest and the one that deserves the most attention. Here is where managers need to believe in the strength of the existing organizational climate and culture (assuming it is healthy) to have a powerful impact on new people. As discussed earlier, the sources of commitment can complement and supplement each other; conflict among them may often occur, but this is not inevitable nor unresolvable. Recognize and build on the commitment that new employees bring to the organization (identification with the work), provide opportunities for them to further reinforce that commitment, and make sure that it is also connected to the organization's goals and people, which is the only sure way to extend identification into the system itself.

One word of caution: People become part of a social system through *enculturation*. Enculturation, if it occurs in a healthy way, allows for individuality as well as commonality of needs. If a social system *indoctrinates* its members, it is overlooking individuality in favor of homogeneity; if it *educates* its members, it is teaching them the customs and norms of the system but encouraging individual development within those customs and norms. Consequently, new people are *integrated* and not *assimilated;* the system changes and grows with the new blood, rather than modifying the new to fit the old.

This is especially important today, as organizations become more and more knowledge-based, need to attract strong individual talents, and consequently have to find ways to create a *mutual* fit between the customs of the past and the patterns of the future. This is difficult enough in organizations that recruit exclusively from the bottom and connect enculturation to advancement (and vice versa). Increasing demands, usually related to technological advances, to hire new people at middle and higher levels of the organization, complicate the picture. How is it possible to create a healthy fit between the personal styles of new people hired into positions of relative power and the overall style of the organization? It is not sensible to screen out the best talent because they do not fit; but neither is it desirable to destroy the organization's culture, if it is vital and supportive of success, to accommodate special talent. It is hoped that managers are not faced with this dilemma too often, but there are times when it cannot be avoided. Therefore, it is important to consider several courses of action.

First, recognize that most organizational cultures are not easily changed or even shaken up very much. Second, some highly talented people come packaged in highly distinct personalities and are best accepted as such. Third, creating a special niche for such individuals in the organization accomplishes several objectives:

1. The company will have that special talent as a resource.
2. The organization will be enriched with something it had not previously possessed.
3. The company will communicate to others an acceptance of deviation from the norm and a respect for individuality. This encourages others to behave in kind and to discourage conformity for the sake of preserving the status quo.
4. The company will foster an atmosphere that supports diversity, which will in turn encourage initiative and entrepreneurship, commodities so badly needed by organizations in the coming years.

Dealing with Retrenchment

Retrenchment means cutting back, cutting back means managing scarce resources, and scarce resources lead to a mentality of self-protection and territoriality. What typically happens, then, is that managers retain tight control over information and decision-making, which in turn lowers the level of trust among people. While there seems to be an inherent logic in managers operating to protect their areas (budgets, space, people, and equipment), the unfortunate consequence of all this self-protection is likely to be that everyone loses. What is needed, ironically, is less self-protection and more attention to the overall survival of the enterprise. Furthermore, what is needed above all is the commitment of everyone to the broadest possible goals of the organization rather than to the competing goals of individuals or groups. Creating an atmosphere of secrecy only generates competition for information and, at best, compliance with directives that seem to have no clear rationale.

So how does one go about maintaining or even enhancing people's commitment to their work and to the organization when the deck seems stacked? I would suggest trying some of the following, even if some seem risky.

1. *Share information fully.* I am referring to all the available information relevant to the circumstances, including potentially threatening information, like the possibility of eliminating jobs. The fact is, rumors and fantasy tend to fill information gaps rapidly and destructively. Managers might as well be open and straight with people right from the start. First of all, they will respect a manager for it, and the manager will certainly need that respect to maintain credibility. Secondly, they will feel trusted and will tend to honor that trust by putting forth their best efforts. Third, information sharing generates interaction, and interaction helps to maintain cohesiveness, which is certainly needed in times of adversity. If the cohesiveness extends through the total system, the collective energies of all employees work in the same direction. The common enemy is external (usually other companies), not internal, where it has divisive effects.

Even budgetary decisions can be shared to a greater extent than one might think. Share the total financial picture with immediate subordinates, and encourage them to do the same for their budgets with their subordinates. Managers will find that such an act of empowerment generates a willingness to cooperate and to engage in a true sharing of scarce resources.

2. *Turn the situation into a challenge.* Sometimes that worst crisis becomes an opportunity to make some creative and often long overdue changes. It may seem at first like fighting an uphill battle because people usually find it hard to be creative when their fears about survival are high. However, tension is energy, and energy can be mobilized. If a manager has followed my first suggestion, which is necessary for this one to work, employees will be sharing a common life raft and a common goal to survive. The mutual support they feel will generate an esprit de corps that can release creative thought. Brainstorming can be a tremendously valuable tool at this point. Set aside a block of time and have a group of employees, or even several groups, brainstorm ideas on such matters as:

1. How to minimize costs
2. How to make better use of existing resources
3. How to generate new resources.

From their ideas a manager will discover some new ways of doing things or better ways to organize that might never have arisen under normal circumstances. The process will foster everyone's commitment, but the manager had better not drop the ball there. Once the process is started, it is imperative, for the manager's future credibility to make sure that some of the ideas are implemented. And let those who are most closely associated with those ideas carry the main responsibility for their implementation. In that way a manager can engender their maximum commitment.

3. *Generate a winning group mentality.* There is no more debilitating situation than that faced by a group that sees itself as a losing group. This is the picture presented by the defeated player profile. The members of the group continually blame either each other or some outside factor for their failures, and they seem to get a perverse sense of satisfaction in displaying their losing qualities to the world. The self-fulfilling prophecy they foster becomes very difficult to reverse. Groups or organizations in crisis often feel defeated and develop a losing group mentality. If managers see signs of this in their own settings, including their own attitudes, it is time to turn things around.

Start by identifying an objective that is positive and reachable. It may amount to something as small as one percent fewer defective parts, or ten more clients served, or some very minimal (but measurable) increase in production. The important thing is to have a very clear and measurable goal that, once attained, serves as a signal to people that they can make things better.

A measured success, however small, serves to disconfirm the self-fulfilling prophecy, helps to rebuild cohesiveness, and starts the momentum going in the direction of success, eventually generating a winning group mentality. But to make this succeed managers need to believe in their abilities to turn the situation around.

Commitment and Financial Control

Nothing generates more tension, competition, and power struggles than budgeting. Money becomes equated with power, and power is seen as a scarce commodity. The allocation of financial resources usually is defined as a zero-sum game in which one person's gain is another's loss. The result is an endless series of cautious bargaining in which everyone assumes that everyone else is out to get the maximum, no matter who else might suffer. This kind of scenario is hardly conducive to generating collective commitment to the enterprise as a whole. Individuals and groups lose sight of the whole as they narrowly focus on their own limited goals.

While it is not easy to break the pattern, I strongly suggest that those currently caught up in it take drastic and dramatic steps to change it. It will feel risky, especially if business is slow, but it will result ultimately in great savings in both dollars and time, not to mention aggravation.

1. Share and delegate financial control.
2. Keep financial information accurate and available to key managers.

3. Encourage—or even require—key managers to share and discuss their financial needs with each other and to negotiate among themselves for scarce resources.

4. Do not let managers engage in one-on-one secret bargaining with the top executive.

5. Encourage managers to be inventive about how to share financial resources and how to multiply the payoff for expenditures.

All these steps represent acts of trust that will enhance commitment to the top executive and others in the system and will result in joint ownership of the activities that the budget supports. And finally, it will turn out that a more open system of budget management is more economical in every respect.

Let me cite an example. A number of years ago I consulted with a medium-sized manufacturing firm in England. At the time, it was going through what seemed like a major crisis, and the level of tension was very high. The managing director was sharing with me his fears about the financial situation and asked my advice on how he should deal with each of his subordinates. His concern was that each would make budget requests such that when all were added together, the result would be far beyond what the company could handle. His usual pattern was to negotiate with each manager separately and behind closed doors. It was also his policy that the managers not discuss their budget requests with each other. In previous years his worst fears had always been confirmed, and he had to go through the laborious process of repeated meetings with the managers until the budget was balanced. This time he wanted to try something different.

What I suggested was that he delegate the entire budgeting process to his managers and that he stay out of it. At first he thought my idea was absurd, but he decided that since the old way did not work very well, he had little to lose by trying something different, even at the risk of handing over control. A week later the group of managers came back to the managing director with a finished budget proposal that showed a surplus. They explained to him that when they could look at the total picture, trust that no games were being played, and had complete access to all financial information, they had made it their goal to create a company surplus.

I cannot promise that this process would work in every situation, but my own experience tells me that a policy of secrecy in financial matters almost never works in the best interests of the organization.

Managing Conflicting Commitments

One manager recently told me about a situation in his department that illustrated how commitment can have some negative consequences. One of his best employees had reached a point in her career where she was ready to move on to a more responsible and challenging position, a move that would have been good for her own development and good for the organization.

She chose to remain in her current job because she felt a very strong commitment to both her co-workers and her boss.

He was not sure what to do at first. He valued her loyalty and the effort she always put into her work, but he also realized that ultimately she would regret the decision to stay put. He also felt that the company could really benefit from her talents. He put pressure on her to leave the nest, which she finally did, but not happily.

In a situation like this, and I know they occur frequently, it is important to establish some priorities and to make every effort to reward behavior related to the priorities. If the organization is one that encourages employee development and provides career ladders for people, it is possible for managers to foster commitment to goals that go beyond their own departments. If the connections between the individual's efforts and the goals of the system are repeatedly reinforced, it will help that person maintain a sense of identification with corporate mission and not just personal or departmental goals.

In a similar way, successful design or redesign of jobs, making them more intrinsically rewarding and closely reflective of individual goals, is fine up to a point. It can create a problem if that is the only source of commitment. It can generate an individualistic performer profile, in which employees may be ready to jump companies because they are committed only to the work and wholly indifferent to the setting and the people with whom they work.

The Uses of Physical Space

Physical space in an organization has both operational and symbolic meaning. The operational aspects of space clearly affect the ways in which people carry out their work. Space affects individual comfort and convenience, opportunities for contact with others, and ease of access to important sources of information and people. As discussed in Chapter 11, it also has a significant impact on the relations among groups in an organization. In these respects, space allocations have powerful effects on productivity and satisfaction, but may or may not affect commitment very much. I suspect that poor spatial arrangements can impose such constraints on employees that their levels of job commitment are likely to suffer. However, the ways in which space is likely to increase commitment are more related to the symbolic aspects of its use.

I knew one manager who talked a great deal about the importance of employee participation in decisions, but always made sure that the most attractive spaces in the company (near windows with a nice view, easy access to sucy conveniences as rest rooms and elevators) were reserved for the most important people, including himself. This is a common practice among managers and may even be considered a desirable part of the rewards of a company. If that is the choice and there is no compelling reason to change the practice, be aware that decisions regarding the use of space communicate something to employees. In this example the decisions represented a contradiction of the participative philosophy of management.

In contrast, Fritz Steele consulted with a company in which he advised the president to reserve prime space as a common area for all employees. The result was that employees at a number of different levels in the company had frequent contact, shared information and perceptions, learned something about areas of the company they rarely saw, and generally increased their personal senses of being part of a whole system. This certainly can foster both interpersonal and organizational commitment—and in this example it did. The symbolism in identifying the most attractive space as shared space was a powerful message which said that everyone was important enough to share some of the special benefits.

In general, I would suggest the following guidelines in the allocation of physical space:

1. Assign areas in ways that facilitate the flow of information, the movement of products or service, and the accessibility of those combinations of people needed for ongoing decisions.

2. Once the requirements are defined, create the necessary combinations of people to negotiate all other aspects of space allocations.

Any tendency of managers to compete for prime space or plush offices reflects an internally competitive and politicized system. It fosters self-serving behavior and works against identification with peers and the overall organization. Reserving prime space for sharing and enjoyment by many employees conveys to all employees their worth to the organization.

The Importance of Rituals and Ceremonies

We surround so many important events in our lives with rituals and ceremonies—weddings, graduation, retirement—why not enhance the importance of events at work with some of the same attention? Many organizations may use ceremonies as a substitute for something substantive; employees often see such events as trivial and meaningless. Commitment is not generated or sustained by such acts. Rituals or ceremonies, to mean something, must be related to important events in the life of the company or in the lives of its members. To celebrate the success of a new product, becoming number one in the industry, the unveiling of some innovation, or just surviving the struggle of the first year of business can provide a stamp of approval and a sense of pride in accomplishment. This can help to reinforce and further build people's commitment to their work, each other, and the organization.

The Davidson Instrument Panel division of Textron Corporation recently celebrated "Zero Defects Day," which symbolizes a commitment of the company and its employees to a goal of zero defects in product manufacturing at the Farmington, New Hampshire, plant. The plant, which employs about eight hundred people, is dedicated to becoming a world class operation by involving all employees in teams that essentially manage themselves and take full responsibility for the maintenance of quality. An article in the local newspaper described the event as a half-day celebration of the collective efforts of all employees and as an opportunity for them to rededicate themselves to the level of quality represented in the goal of zero defects.

There is celebration beyond description in the sports world. Whole cities go berserk when their teams win pennants or championships. Nations stop what they are doing to join in celebration of Olympic gold medals. If the joy of life can be expressed so freely in sports, why not in our everyday work? Commitment is a form of bonding—people to work, people to each other, and people to their institutions. I would advise organizations to look at their rituals and ceremonies. Are they arbitrary and scheduled in some convenient way throughout the year so as not to interfere with work? Or are they directly and clearly connected to the mission, goals, and work of the organization and its people? The latter makes a real difference in the level of commitment found in any given setting.

Sustaining Commitment during a Crisis

While some degree of tension or pressure can serve as a stimulus for action and as a source of psychological energy, and while too little tension or pressure can lead to lethargy and indifference, too much can result in dysfunctional behavior. When people are under excessive stress, especially for a long period of time, the ability to reason effectively is diminished, they start to focus on only short-term decisions, look for ways to reduce tension as quickly as possible (at the expense of genuine problem-solving), seek to take control over what otherwise might be trusted to others to manage, deal with others in ways that create difficulties, and, in general, operate in a survival mode that tends to create more problems than it solves.

Organizations today are operating in a world of tremendous turmoil and uncertainty. Inevitably it produces crisis-like behavior inside those organizations. Instead of managing the uncertainty, people focus on avoiding or reducing immediate tension. Managers often resort more and more to unilateral control, believing that it is the best way to take charge. They become heroic fighter pilots who forget that they are part of a team flying a jumbo jet.

The bottom line is that it is very difficult, perhaps even paradoxical, to maintain the attitudes and behavior that build employee commitment when one's instincts are to exercise maximum control over events and people. But that is precisely what managers must do, despite the sense of risk they might feel, if the organization is to survive and grow. What it amounts to is operating in an almost counter-intuitive way.

I sometimes believe that we struggle with this issue all our lives, trying to maintain the feeling of being grounded while we walk a tightrope. I remember the times my wife watched our three-year-old daughter climb a set of monkey bars for the first time. Her instinct was to hold on to her, but her understanding of the child's need to conquer the challenge kept her from being too protective. I have known many managers who find it difficult to give their employees the freedom to climb the organizational monkey bars and consequently stifle the employees' development.

I would suggest that employees' commitment in all three dimensions is even more critical in times of crisis than at any other times. Because employees take their behavior cues from those in power, it behooves management to set the tone for effective behavior during crises. It also behooves management to understand that the same situation can be experienced very differently by different people. What one individual perceives to be threatening, another might not. Someone else's overreaction in the manager's eyes might, through that person's eyes, be a perfectly understandable reaction to a given situation. The calm manager who has control over events may be puzzled by the distraught behavior of the employee who does not.

More than ever, organizations today are undergoing major changes, even transformations. As discussed in the first few chapters of this book, new structures are being tried, new styles of leadership fostered, and work is being redesigned to make it more varied and challenging. Consequently, many employees feel a great sense of uncertainty about when and where all the changes will end, if ever, and just how well they will survive it all. Fears about losing valued work relationships or having to form new ones not freely chosen, anxiety about having to learn new skills that may make one feel foolish and incompetent, expectations that the demands will increase and make work life more difficult than ever, are just a few examples that generate a sense of personal crisis for many employees.

In one manufacturing plant of a supplier of parts to the Big Three automakers, major efforts have been initiated to move the plant to a team-centered style of management, right down to the shop floor. As part of this effort a major training program was put in place to teach supervisors team leadership skills and to change their roles from direct supervisors to team facilitators. It was not surprising to find a vast array of reactions to this program, from enthusiasm to blatant refusal to cooperate. Those who were enthusiastic obviously perceived little threat in the change and felt some degree of confidence in their own abilities to learn the skills and change their roles.

At the other extreme were those who felt that they had done things a certain way for all their working years and saw no need to change; besides, they were probably too old to learn the new ways. The latter group is not atypical of what one finds in any organization undergoing fundamental changes. But often there is a lack of understanding and compassion on the part of the initiators of the change for the kind of crisis these employees are likely to be experiencing. It is not that they really do not see the importance of the changes, but more that they cannot see themselves in the changed roles and behaving in unfamiliar ways. It is threatening; it is, for them, a personal crisis.

However, from all that we know about the ways in which people work their way through life's crises, including such serious events as the loss of a loved one, a permanent disability, the loss of job, or a divorce, people do find within themselves the resources to make the changes, to eventually cope effectively with crisis. What starts out as an overwhelming threat eventually becomes a major challenge. The steps along the way can be strenuous and at times discouraging, but usually the sense of mastery one finally experiences can offset and compensate for that struggle.

Even what appear from the outside to be very minor changes can be felt by an individual to be stressful. I once had a secretary who let a word processor sit in its unopened box on the floor for nearly a year, fearful that she would make a fool of herself if she even attempted to learn to use it. When she did finally overcome her resistance and accept the challenge, she became very enthusiastic about her new skills and wondered why everyone did not have a word processor. Not an unfamiliar story.

In all these examples of change the initial stages seemed to be marked by some degree of compliance to work requirements, eventually ending in strong commitment to the new behavior. It may just be that we cannot really know if we like a new suit of clothes until we have tried it on and actually worn it for a while. It can be helpful to employees struggling with change over which they feel little control to be given the opportunity to try the behavior on and see how it fits before being expected to feel committed to it.

A number of years ago I was in charge of a segment of a program that was preparing Peace Corps volunteers to enter a country in the Middle East. Because culture shock was known to be a serious problem for Peace Corps volunteers in that part of the world, those in charge of the training placed strong emphasis on this aspect of the program. Certainly people cannot be prepared for such an experience by being lectured to or told to read about and discuss the problem. They need to experience it for themselves, to some extent at least.

We created a series of events at the training site that simulated the circumstances that tend to produce culture shock, events designed to force the trainees to cope with things outside their control. The point of the exercise was to generate the unexpected feelings that usually occur when one is thrown into a foreign culture and to allow the individuals to learn to manage their way through these feelings. One very important thing that most discovered was that they had no advance sense of just how much of a crisis they would experience. Letters from many of them after they went overseas indicated that they did experience in even more dramatic ways many of the same problems and feelings that the training generated, but that the training at least made those feelings familiar and easier to manage.

Employees, managers, and workers alike very often do not know in advance just what a change will be like, only to discover after the fact that it was a lot more difficult than expected. This can produce a feeling of being overwhelmed by the pressures. Although advance knowledge that this is likely to occur, such as the Peace Corps volunteers had, will not stop it from happening, it does give people a sense that what they are experiencing is normal, that they have been there before, and that they can get through it now. Support and encouragement help people manage their way through crises; anger, impatience, and disparagement do not.

Sustaining employees' commitment in times of crisis is, in the final analysis, a matter of fighting the survival tendencies that generate controlling behavior and short-term thinking; it is, instead, a matter of increasing the involvement of others and maintaining a long-term perspective.

Balancing Work and Personal Life

For a number of years, especially during the 1970s, it looked like organizations were making great strides toward shorter work weeks, flexible working arrangements, and a variety of new ways to help employees improve the quality of their lives through a better balance between work life and personal life. The fact is that people are working 15 to 20 percent longer now than they did in 1970, and the pressures on managers to spend more time at work have only increased. When flextime was adopted by many organizations, it opened the door for many women to enter the work force who otherwise had inflexible responsibilities at home with small children—and nowadays with aging parents. Those same women, especially those in management, now are experiencing increasing conflicts in how they manage their time and how they can be in two places at once. Single male parents (whose numbers also seem to be increasing) also are struggling with the same problems.

Commitment to one's job and commitment to one's family have a history of inherent conflict. I am not referring to commitment in the sense of loyalty, the transactional expectation on the part of the organization that one is expected to make the job the primary focus of one's waking life if one expects to get ahead. In some sense the choice there is clear. What I am referring to here is the dilemma one feels as a result of having such a strong identification with the job, including the people and the setting itself, that one establishes no boundaries between oneself as employee and as family member. One finds oneself living and breathing work to the point that family and friends find one inaccessible physically and, worse, psychologically. The consequences are fairly predictable: burnout, divorce, physical and psychological problems, addictions in one form or another, deterioration of one's actual performance, and eventually the possibility of losing the very job to which one is committed.

In the days when management equated loyalty with time spent on the job and the employee's willingness to drop everything else for the sake of the company, it was easy for those who bought the package to justify their actions because they did not make the rules that determined their career paths. When the culprit is the employee, whose own internalization of the organization's values is the driving force behind the behavior, the struggle is much more difficult because it involves conflicts between internal values.

Organizations that cannot let go of the compliance mode of management, which sustains the belief that the best way to measure an employee's performance is to clock his or her time on the job, will never foster true commitment, but neither will they create the dilemma of those companies that do foster it, the overcommitted worker. However, many organizations have found some interesting and effective ways to deal with the dilemma. Companies like Liberty Mutual and Pacific Bell, as well as many others, have increased the number of employees who work out of their homes. Computer technology has become the savior of those people who otherwise would have been forced to drop out of the labor force. Stride-Rite has provided not only day care for the children of its employees but has gone so far as to provide on-site care for aging parents who require supervision.

It takes an entirely new way of thinking about people and work for any organization to move in these directions. As discussed in the section on managing in crisis, managers today are feeling the pressures and the stress of turbulence in the outside environment, as well as constant change from within. These factors do not make it easy for them to think in terms of time away from work or the costs of day care or entrusting employees to take the responsibility of managing their own work at home. Such actions run counter to the sense of having control over events. Ironically, however, it is precisely those kinds of actions that help generate commitment and, consequently, result in the highest levels of productivity and development in the organization.

Teaching Commitment

One cannot actually teach or train people to be committed to their work, co-workers, or the organization. In fact, the act of actually teaching, in the traditional sense, is likely to have the opposite effect of that intended. What one can do is create a learning environment in which participants engage in activities for which they take responsibility and then reflect on the impact of the experience. Identification is a psychological process that occurs over time under the right conditions; it is not a method or technique taught in a classroom hour.

What I find to be the most important aspect of the learning process, if it is to result in commitment, is that the learner must take the major responsibility for managing that process. This is obviously not a new idea, since the world's best educators are those who empower their students to learn from the heart, from self-generated drive. Therefore, to produce education that strengthens commitment, be careful not to overdesign the activity. Create broad boundaries for learning, making clear the "vision" for the outcomes, but give participants all the room they need to manage their own education within those boundaries. A lockstep activity with predetermined outcomes produces compliant behavior, not committed behavior. Whatever content is learned, the more powerful message comes from the way it was learned. It is possible for highly charismatic teachers to engender strong personal identification to the point where the students feel enthusiastic about what they are teaching. But that should not be mistaken for the kind of self-directed learning that comes from self-management. A beloved supervisor can get employees to work hard, but that does not result in love of the work itself, of co-workers, or of the organization.

Let me give a brief example of a workshop I have used to "teach" the value of commitment. It is called "The Sentence Factory," and it simply involves creating an organization (ten to thirty people in a classroom setting) that produces sentences from little blocks of letters on strips glued to larger sheets of paper to form a sentence that has been determined in advance.

The traditional organization is demonstrated by having participants organized into an assembly line, each with a specified task, and with a single supervisor managing the production process. The larger the group the more assembly lines one can set up. The production process usually runs fifteen to twenty minutes. With more than one assembly line, some level of competition always develops.

After the first round of production the group (or groups) is told that it now can redesign the way it conducts its work and it can create its own sentences. Also, it can feel free to eliminate the role of supervisor (which almost every group does). After the second production run the groups are asked to discuss and report how they experienced the two different ways of working and to generate a list of principles learned from the experience. It does not take much imagination to predict the outcomes, and it certainly would take less time and be more efficient to simply present a lecture that states the same principles. That might have filled some notebook paper, but it would never have produced internalized learning, identification with the process itself.

I am sure everyone can find an almost infinite variety of exercises like the one just described and that one might even want to invent some. The important thing to keep in mind with respect to training is the same thing that any manager needs to keep in mind when managing: To generate a high level of employee commitment, set the stage, get out of the way, and let people manage themselves.

Concluding Thoughts

Any organization that wishes to build a high commitment system needs to understand where that system is on the continuum of levels of commitment. Whether one uses a specific diagnostic method such as the CDI or more observational techniques like commitment indicators, diagnostic steps should always precede any interventions.

The difficulties imposed by entering a period of organizational diagnosis are many, including the fears of employees about the motives of management, raised expectations that might never be met, a sense of familiarity that may border on cynicism, and a variety of other issues that might distort the information obtained in the diagnosis. All are an inevitable part of the process of change and need to be managed with sensitivity and patience. However, there is one added element present in a diagnosis of commitment levels, particularly in the use of an instrument like the CDI. Instead of being viewed as a means of understanding the organization and the needs of its employees, it can easily be considered a form of employee evaluation that leads to judgments about the quality of the employees themselves. This cannot be avoided completely, especially in organizations where the relationship between the upper and lower levels of the system is lacking in trust. Employees are likely to be concerned more about how they *should* respond to questions than about being totally honest. Even attempts to guarantee anonymity can be futile.

To the extent that management acts promptly to improve things based upon the diagnostic information, its credibility in the eyes of employees will rise and subsequent data gathering will produce better and better information. The cycle, often called the *action-research cycle,* should continue and become an ongoing part of management practices. Then, what gets reinforced in the eyes of employees is the belief that the intent of the data gathering is improving the organization and not assessing them as individuals.

Because commitment results from identification, it follows that the management of an organization that is attempting to build commitment ought to share ownership of the process with its employees. This can be done by providing employees with the means of assessing their own levels of commitment, allowing them to conduct their own diagnoses, and ultimately designing for themselves the changes that need to occur to foster commitment in .all three categories. We are witnessing the emergence of self-managing work teams; why not develop self-managing change teams? Such an approach represents a consistency between the desired ends and the means to achieve those ends. The ultimate outcome, then, will be a *high commitment workplace.*

Appendix A

Means and Distributions of CDI Scores for the Research Samples

The means and distributions of the CDI scores are reported for the total combined samples from the two companies (N = 848) and then for the subsamples of managers (N = 325) and operational (hourly) employees (N = 499). In reviewing these data it is possible to compare any scores (individual, group, or organizational) one has obtained using the CDI with whatever grouping is relevant. Although the samples come from manufacturing firms, which may raise some question as to their translation to other, more service-oriented industries, most items in the CDI pertain to very general human behavior and attitudes that occur in any organizational context. This would be especially true for people in management, where the problems are not too dissimilar from one industry to another.

Total Sample

Figure A.1 shows the distribution of CDI total scores for the 848 individuals in the combined samples from companies A and B. The mean total commitment score was 114.5; the cutoff points for the bottom 25 percent and top 25 percent respectively, were 102 and 130. In the identification with work category (see Figure A.2), the mean was 39.7, and the lower and upper 25 percent cutoff points were 34 and 45. (The scores for each category can easily be translated into the original item range by dividing the score by 10. For example, a score of 34 translates into 3.4 on the 0–6 rating scale, which says that the 34 falls slightly above the middle of the range. To apply the same procedure to the total CDI score, divide by 30 the total number of items.) In the co-worker category (see Figure A.3), the mean commitment score was 37.5, with lower and upper 25 percent cutoffs of 33 and 42. In the organizational commitment area (see Figure A.4), the mean was 37.0, and the cutoffs were 31 and 43.

Management Sample

Of the total sample from the two companies, 325 people were in salaried management positions ranging from first-line to upper middle managers. Figure A.5 shows the distribution of CDI total scores for that group. The mean score was 122, the lower 25 percent cutoff point was 112, and the upper 25 percent cutoff was 134. In the work commitment category (see Figure A.6), the mean was 41.5, with lower and upper cutoff points of 36 and 46, respectively. In the co-worker area (see Figure A.7), the mean was 39.4, with lower and upper cutoffs of 35 and 44. In the organizational commitment category (see Figure A.8), the mean was 40.6 and the lower and upper 25 percent cutoffs were 35 and 45, respectively.

Operational Employee Sample

This group was composed of 499 hourly employees working in technical and support functions in the companies. Figure A.9 shows the distribution of CDI total scores for that group. The mean CDI total score was 110, the lower 25 percent cutoff point was 96, and the top 25 percent cutoff was 126. In the work commitment category (see Figure A.10), the mean was 38.4, and the lower and upper 25 percent cutoffs were 33 and 44, respectively. For commitment to co-workers (see Figure A.11), the mean was 37.0, and the lower and upper cutoffs were 32 and 41. In the organizational commitment area (see Figure A.12), the mean was 34.9, the lower 25 percent cutoff was 29, and the upper was 41.

Company Sample Comparisons

Chapter 5 reported the results of comparisons of means from the two companies as a whole, as well as the means of the management and operational employee samples separately. Presented here are the distributions of those samples. However, to save the reader the trouble of having to go back to Chapter 5 to find the means of the samples or the results of the tests for significant differences, that information is provided again.

Total CDI Scores

Figure A.13 shows the distribution of the 418 total CDI scores obtained from the sample at Company A. Figure A.14 shows that same distribution for the sample of 430 from Company B. The mean for Company A was 116.8 and that for Company B was 112.2. The difference was significant beyond the 1 percent level of confidence.

Commitment to Work Scores

Figures A.15 and A.16 show the distributions of scores for each company respectively in the work identification category. The mean score for Company A was 40.5 and that for Company B was 38.9. The difference was not statistically significant.

Commitment to Co-Workers Scores

Figures A.17 and A.18 show the distributions for the scores in the category of co-worker identification for the two companies. The mean for Company A was 37.0 and for Company B it was 38.0. The difference between the two was not significant.

Organizational Commitment Scores

Figures A.19 and A.20 show the distribution of scores for each company in the category of organizational commitment. The means for Companies A and B were 39.0 and 35.0, respectively, which were significantly different well beyond the 1 percent confidence level.

Figure A.1. CDI–Total Score Distribution (N = 848)

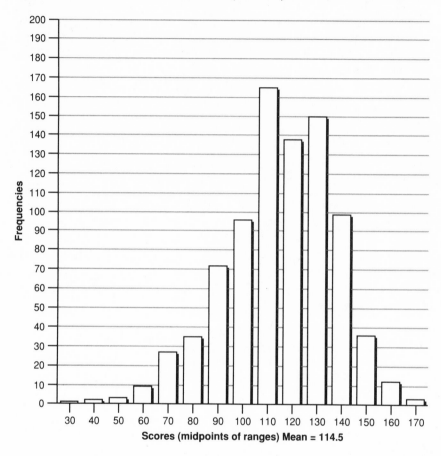

Figure A.2. CDI–Work Score Distribution (N = 848)

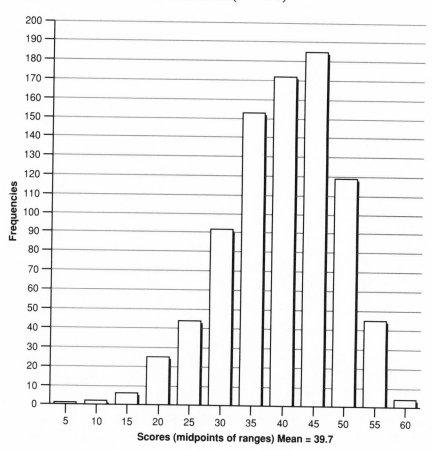

Figure A.3. CDI–Co-Worker Score Distribution (N = 848)

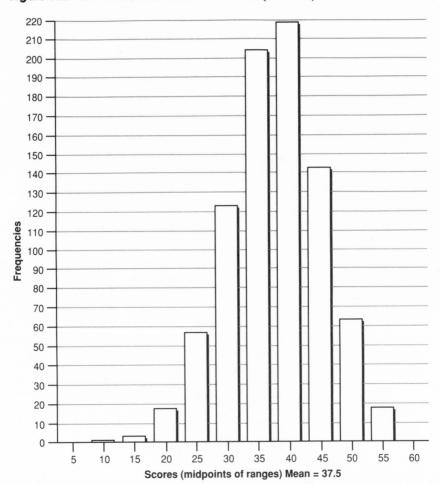

Figure A.4. CDI–Organization Score Distribution (N = 848)

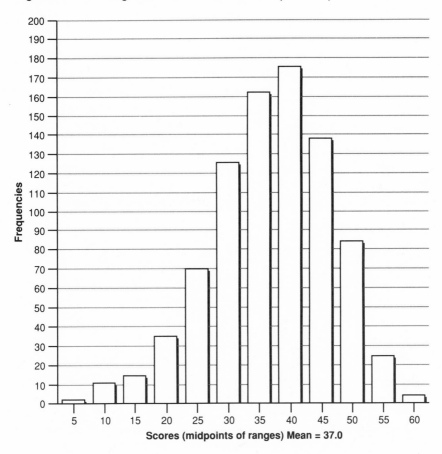

Figure A.5. Distribution of Total CDI Scores: Management (N = 325)

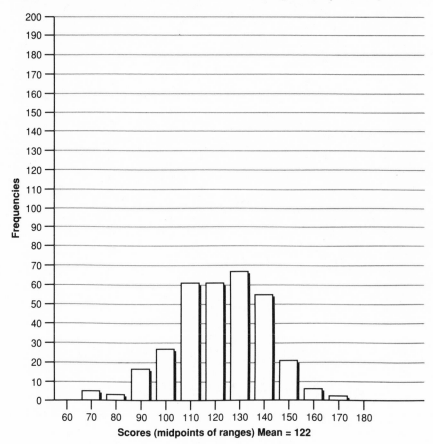

Figure A.6. Distribution of CDI–Work Scores: Management (N = 325)

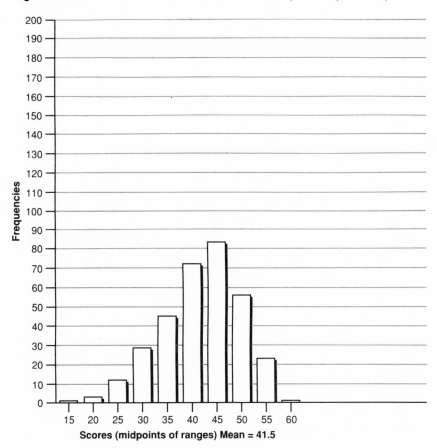

Figure A.7. Distribution of CDI–Co-Worker Scores: Management (N = 325)

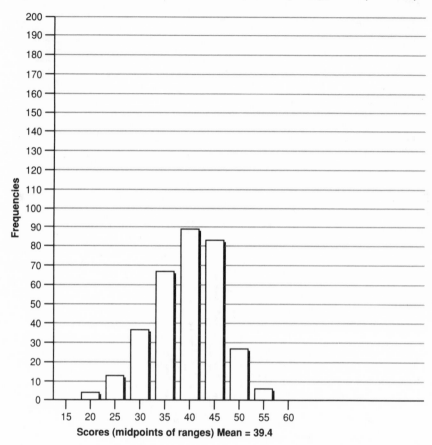

Figure A.8. Distribution of CDI–Organization Scores: Management (N = 325)

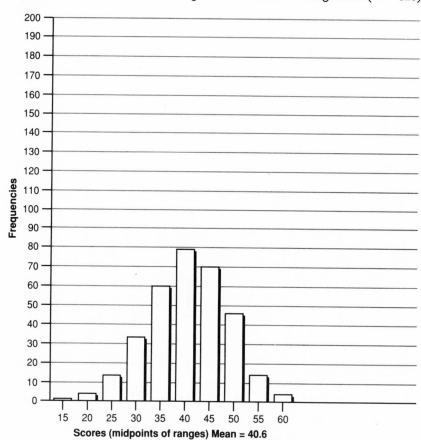

Figure A.9. Distribution of Total CDI Scores: Operational Employees (N = 499)

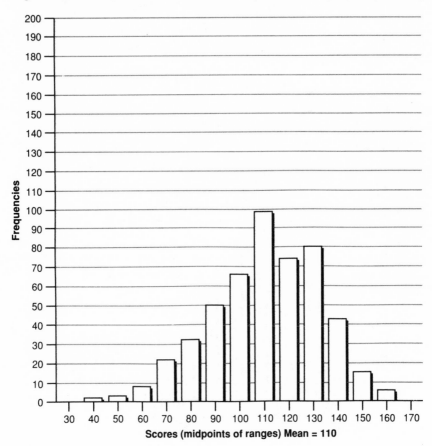

Figure A.1O. Distribution of CDI–Work Scores: Operational Employees (N = 499)

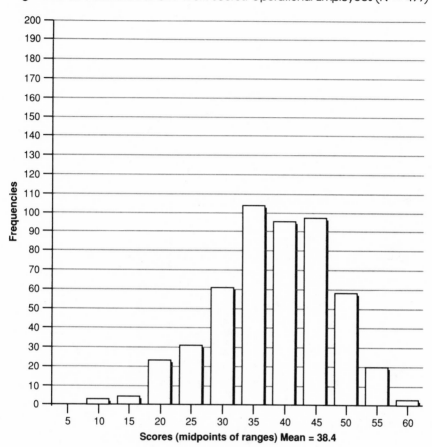

Figure A.11. Distribution of CDI–Co-Worker Scores: Operational Employees (N = 499)

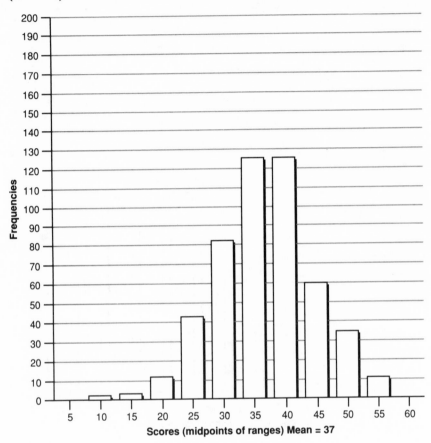

Figure A.12. Distribution of CDI–Organization Scores: Operational Employees (N = 499)

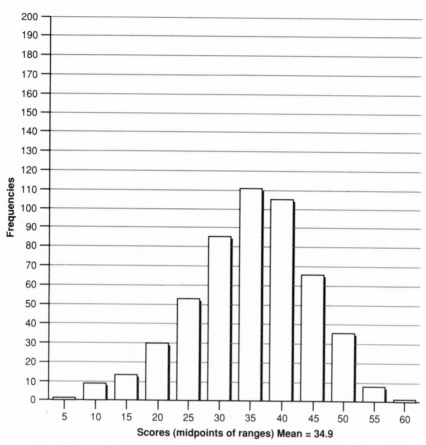

Figure A.13. CDI–Total Score Distribution for Company A (N = 418)

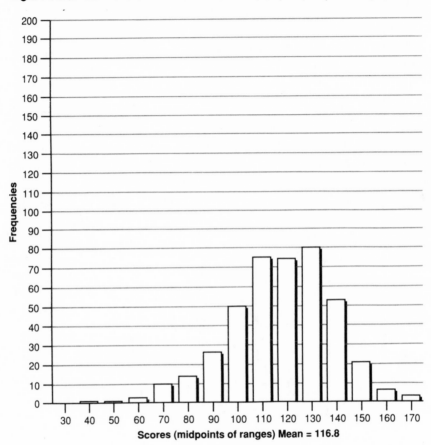

Figure A.14. CDI–Total Score Distribution for Company B (N = 430)

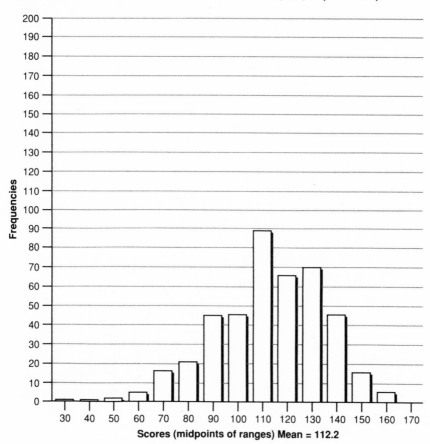

Figure A.15. CDI–Work Score Distribution for Company A (N = 418)

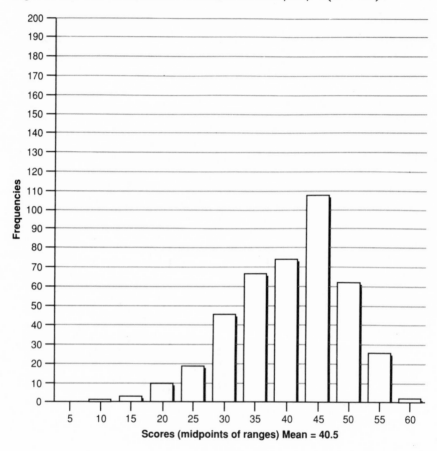

Figure A.16. CDI–Work Score Distribution for Company B (N = 430)

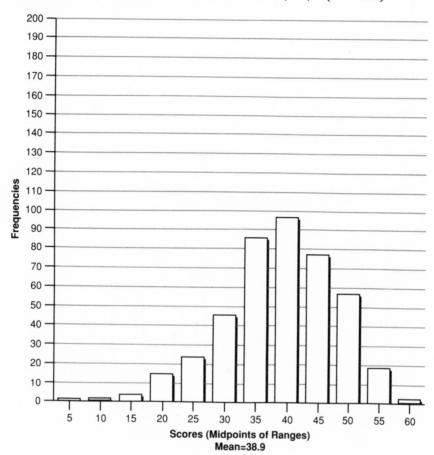

Scores (Midpoints of Ranges)
Mean=38.9

Figure A.17. CDI–Co-Worker Score Distribution for Company A (N = 418)

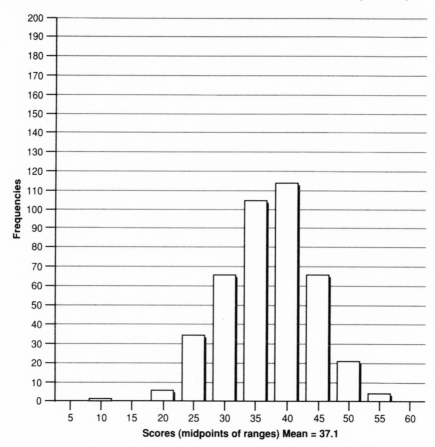

Figure A.18. CDI–Co-Worker Score Distribution for Company B (N = 430)

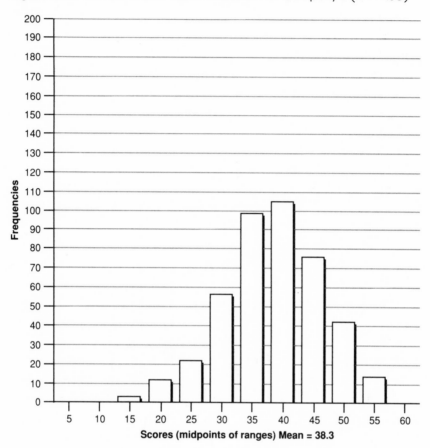

Figure A.19. CDI–Organization Score Distribution for Company A (N = 418)

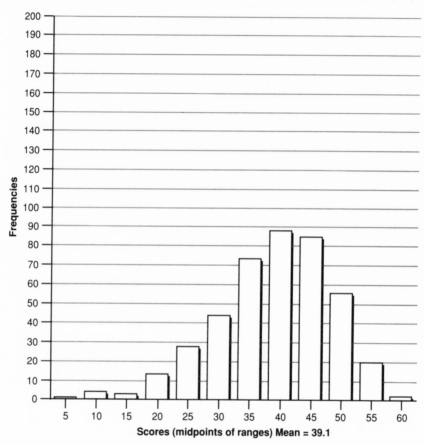

Scores (midpoints of ranges) Mean = 39.1

Figure A.20. CDI–Organization Score Distribution for Company B (N = 430)

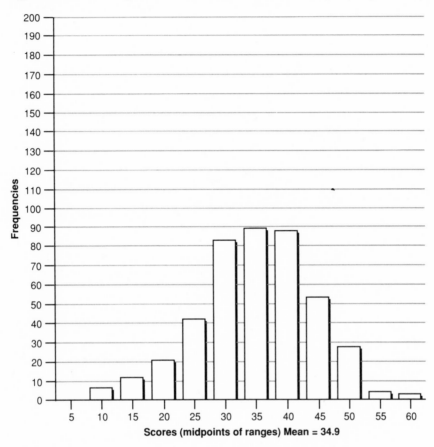

Appendix B

Some Basic Statistical Concepts

Means and Distributions

The most frequent use of statistics is to describe data. What one usually wants to know about a set of scores is its distribution and its mean. These pieces of information are especially important in the kind of research presented here because users of the CDI need to know how to compare their own or their organization's scores with some set of norms. The user then can determine how far above or below the mean a given score is. What I have chosen to report here is the mean for each CDI category for a number of different groupings of the data and the upper and lower twenty-fifth percentile points for each distribution. This will enable the user to determine a general midrange of scores (middle 50 percent) and two ranges that reflect relatively high and relatively low scores. Although a statistic like the standard deviation is needed to determine other important aspects of the data, it is not conceptually useful to the CDI user; therefore, standard deviations for the distributions are not reported.

Correlations

A correlation between two variables is simply an index of their relationship. If one variable tends to go up as the other goes up, we can say there is a positive correlation; if one goes down as the other goes up, we can say there is a negative correlation. If one picked one hundred people at random and measured their heights and weights, one probably would find a positive correlation between the two. If one also measured how high they could jump, the chances are that there would be a negative correlation between that and weight.

Correlations are very important in the context here. One basic question, for example, pertains to whether a correlation may exist between level of commitment and level of performance. It is expected that the correlation will be positive; if not, the concept is faulty or it is not being measured validly. One would also expect there to be a positive relationship between the number of years spent at an organization and the level of commitment to the organization. However, other factors can contaminate that relationship. For example, longtime employees who have been passed over for promotion many times are likely to be less committed than newer employees who have advanced rapidly; also, companies that tend to promote from within are likely to show a different level of correlation between tenure and commitment than those that hire new people at all levels.

In other words, a correlation is a simple statistic and cannot reflect the complexities of the relationships between variables. When it is statistically significant (which I will explain shortly), it is because the relationship is strong enough to overshadow the effects of other factors.

The index of correlation is called a correlation coefficient. It ranges from +1.00 to −1.00, with the extremes reflecting perfect correlation, positive or negative. A coefficient that equals 0.00 indicates no relationship at all. The question that always needs to be answered is how large a correlation coefficient does one need to obtain to consider it statistically significant, something that did not occur simply by chance. As those who have studied statistics might remember, the smaller the sample (number of observations) the larger the coefficient has to be in order for it to be significant. This stands to reason, because we know it is scientifically unsound to generalize from only a few cases. However, with very large samples it is possible to obtain correlations that are statistically significant but quite low. This kind of result says that there is a relationship between the variables that is better than chance, but that it is up to the investigator to determine just how important that finding is, which is a subjective and often practical matter.

For example, if one finds a correlation coefficient of 0.25 in a sample of one thousand paired observations, one needs to consider the context in which one wishes to use that finding. If the figure represents the predictive power of test scores with respect to grades in the selection of students entering college, it is probably useful to use the test for the thousands of students who apply for admission. But for predicting the success of any given student, or even a small sample of students, the correlation is too low to be of much use, although one still can have confidence that there is a relationship between the test scores and college grades.

Reliability and Validity

One important distinction that needs to be made is the difference between reliability and validity. *Reliability* refers to the consistency of the measure one uses; *validity* refers to whether it is measuring what it is supposed to be measuring. If a set of scores or observations is unreliable, it is not of any use for research or practical purposes. For example, if I administer some kind of test or rating scale to a group of people on one day, repeat it the next, and then find that there is no correlation between the measures from one day to the next, I cannot count on those measures to be reliable for my purposes. Even if I find a significant correlation, but a low one, I would be very uneasy in assuming adequate reliability. Although acceptable figures can vary, depending on the nature of the measures and their purposes, coefficients of at least 0.80 usually reflect acceptable levels of reliability for tests and rating scales that are based on subjective judgments (as with the CDI). Certainly if one were to measure the heights of people on two successive days and found a correlation of only 0.80, one might wonder what was wrong with the measuring instrument or the person using it; reliability in that case should be very close to 1.00, with only slight random errors causing it to fall short of that figure.

In the case of validity the situation is quite different. In this context we need to consider what is called *construct validity,* which refers to the degree to which the instrument (CDI) is really measuring what it is supposed to be measuring (commitment). Insofar as I have carefully defined the concept and systematically translated it into measurable terms, I can justify construct validity. This process is often called *operationalizing the theory.* However, we also need to establish what is called *predictive validity,* which, as the term suggests, refers to the ability of the instrument to predict or at least correlate significantly with some other variable relevant to the purposes of the research. Acceptable validity coefficients also vary depending upon one's purposes, but they are usually much lower than reliability coefficients. In the example of test scores for predicting college grades, the correlation of 0.25 for large numbers of people is acceptable predictive validity, although there are obviously many other factors that affect grades and may even be more useful as predictors. With the sample sizes used in my research (400 +), it is possible to have correlations below 0.20 that are statistically significant at less than a one percent confidence level (noted as $p < 0.01$) and even lower for a five percent confidence level. While such figures might seem useless for practical purposes, they cannot be ignored for research purposes because they do reflect a relationship between two variables that can add to our knowledge of those variables.

It is also important to mention that there are many ways to determine the correlation between two variables and that the different ways often depend upon the assumptions made about the form of the relationship. Is it a simple linear one in which one can assume that a straight line is the best way to depict it? Height and weight have a fairly linear relationship. However, the relationship between some variables is better represented by a curved line than a straight one. For example, if one presses on the gas pedal of a car, the rate of acceleration might be faster at the higher speeds (for some cars anyway) than at the lower speeds. Therefore, if one were to plot the relationship between pressure on the pedal and speed of the car, the correlation would certainly be positive, but not in a straight line. The line would curve upward as one plotted the measures for the higher speeds. Computing a true correlation between pressure and speed in this case would require a more complicated statistical process than that used for simple straight line correlations. For the research I present in this book, I assumed a linear relationship between variables where I use coefficients of correlation.

Differences between Means

If one took two randomly selected samples of men and measured their individual heights, one probably would find some slight difference between the average (mean) heights of the two groups, but a difference that could be explained as a chance occurrence. If one then measured a random sample of women, one probably would find that the average height was considerably shorter than that of the men, for obvious reasons, and one would not need a statistical test to show that. However, if one now wondered whether there was any real difference between the height of the average college student and that of the average blue collar worker, perhaps based upon some theoretical notion, a statistical test could be very important. Suppose, for example, the mean of the college sample was 5 '10 " and that for the workers was 5 '11 ". Is that a difference that one would expect to find simply by chance? A subjective judgment cannot answer that question, but a statistical test can. A test of the significance between the two means takes into account the size of each sample and allows one to determine just how frequently one would find the differences between those means by chance. One can decide for oneself whether five times in a hundred or only once in a hundred is an acceptable level of confidence. In other words, using the example, if the test of significance of the difference between the two means said that the difference would occur by chance only one time in a hundred, one is likely to have confidence (99 percent) that the difference is a real one. If, on the other hand, one learned that the one-inch difference, for the size samples used, could occur as often as ten times in a hundred, one could have less confidence (90 percent) that it is a real difference. For some people 90 percent confidence is not bad, but for most researchers, including me, it is not an acceptable level of significance. In most cases in this book I used a 99 percent confidence level, but also discussed some findings that occurred at a 95 per- cent level.

For those who wish to pursue this material in greater depth, I would suggest a basic text in quantitative analysis.

References

Albrecht, K. *At America's Service*. Homewood, Ill.: Dow Jones-Irwin, 1988.

Angle, H. L., and Perry, J. L. "An Empirical Assessment of Organizational Commitment and Organizational Effectiveness." *Administrative Science Quarterly*, 1981, 26: 1-14.

Bass, B. M. *Leadership and Performance beyond Expectations*. New York: Free Press, 1985.

Bateman, T. S., and Strasser, S. "A Longitudinal Analysis of the Antecedents of Organizational Commitment." *Academy of Management Journal*, 1984, 27: 95-112.

Becker, H. "Notes on the Concept of Commitment." *American Journal of Sociology*, 1960, 66: 32-42.

Benne, K., and Sheats, P. "Functional Roles of Group Members." *Journal of Social Issues*, 1948, 4: 41-49.

Bennis, W., and Nanus, B. *Leaders*. New York: Harper & Row, 1985.

Biggart, N. *Charismatic Capitalism*. Chicago: University of Chicago Press, 1989.

Blake, R. R., and Mouton, J. S. "A Comparative Analysis of Situationalism and 9,9 Management by Principle." *Organizational Dynamics*, Spring 1982: 20-43.

Blau, G. J., and Boal, K. B. "Conceptualizing How Job Involvement and Organizational Commitment Affect Turnover and Absenteeism." *Academy of Management Review*, 1987, 12: 288-300.

Block, P. *The Empowered Manager*. San Francisco: Jossey-Bass, 1987.

Bradford, D. L., and Cohen, A. R. *Managing for Excellence*. New York: John Wiley, 1984.

Brown, M. E. "Identification and Some Conditions of Organizational Involvement." *Administrative Science Quarterly*, 1969, 14: 346-355.

Buchanan, B. "Building Organization Commitment: The Socialization of Managers in Work Organizations." *Administrative Science Quarterly*, 1974, 22: 533-546.

Crampton, W. J., Mowday, R. T., Smith, F. J., and Porter, L.W. "Early Attitudes Predicting Future Behavior: Turnover and Job Performance." Paper presented at the 38th annual meeting of the Academy of Management, San Francisco, August 1978.

Dertouzos, M. L., Lester, R. K., and Solow, R. M. *Made in America*. Cambridge, Mass.: MIT Press, 1989.

Drucker, P. *The Effective Executive*. New York: Harper & Row, 1966.

Galbraith, J. R. *Designing Complex Organizations*. Reading, Mass.: Addison-Wesley, 1973.

――――. *Organization Design*. Reading, Mass.: Addison-Wesley, 1977.

Gardner, J. *On Leadership*. New York: Free Press, 1990.

Gilmore, T. N. *Making a Leadership Change*. San Francisco: Jossey-Bass, 1988.

Gouldner, H. P. "Dimensions of Organizational Commitment." *Administrative Science Quarterly*, 1960, 4: 468–490.

Hackman, J. R., and Lawler, E. E., III. "Employee Reactions to Job Characteristics." *Journal of Applied Psychology Monograph*, 1971, 55: 259–286.

Hackman, J. R., and Oldham, G. R. *Work Redesign*. Reading, Mass.: Addison-Wesley, 1980.

Hall, D. T., Schneider, B., and Nygren, H. T. "Personal Factors in Organizational Identification." *Administrative Science Quarterly*, 1970, 15: 176–189.

Harrison, R. "Role-Negotiation: A Tough-Minded Approach to Team Development." In *Social Technology of Organization Development*. La Jolla, Calif.: University Associates, 1976.

Helgeseñ, S. *The Female Advantage*. New York: Doubleday, 1990.

Heller, J. *Something Happened*. New York: Dell, 1985.

Heller, R. *The Supermanagers*. New York: McGraw-Hill, 1984.

Herman, S. J. G. *Building Company Spirit in Multi-Divisional Organizations*. Doctoral dissertation, School of Education, University of Massachusetts, May 1991.

Herzberg, F., Mausner, B., and Snyderman, B. *The Motivation to Work*. New York: John Wiley, 1959.

Homans, G. *The Human Group*. New York: Harcourt Brace Jovanovich, 1950.

Hrebiniak, L., and Alutto, J. "Personal and Role-Related Factors in the Development of Organizational Commitment." *Administrative Science Quarterly*, 1972, 17: 555–572.

Isgar, T. *The Ten Minute Team*. Boulder, Colo.: Seleura Press, 1989.

Kanter, R. M. "Commitment and Social Organization: A Study of Commitment Mechanisms in Utopian Communities." *American Sociological Review*, 1968, 33: 499–517.

――――, *Commitment and Community: Communes and Utopias in Sociological Perspective*. Cambridge, Mass.: Harvard University Press, 1972.

――――, *The Changemasters*. New York: Simon & Schuster, 1983.

Katz, D. "The Motivational Basis of Organizational Behavior." *Behavioral Science*, 1964, 9: 131–146.

Keidel, R. *Game Plans*. New York: E. P. Dutton, 1985.

Kouzes, J. M., and Posner, B. Z. *The Leadership Challenge*. San Francisco: Jossey-Bass, 1987.

Lewin, K. *Field Theory in Social Science: Selected Papers*. Edited by D. Cartwright. New York: Harper & Row, 1951.

Likert, R. *New Patterns of Management*. New York: McGraw-Hill, 1961.

Luthans, F., McCaul, H. S., and Dodd, N. G. "Organizational Commitment: A Comparison of American, Japanese, and Korean Employees." *Academy of Management Journal*, 1985, 28: 213–219.

Marsh, R. M., and Mannari, M. "Organizational Commitment and Turnover: A Prediction Study." *Administrative Science Quarterly*, 1977, 22: 57–75.

McGregor, D. *The Human Side of Enterprise.* New York: McGraw-Hill, 1960.

Morgan, G. *Images of Organization.* Newbury Park, Calif.: Sage, 1986.

———, *Riding the Waves of Change.* San Francisco: Jossey-Bass, 1988.

Morris, J. H., and Near, J.P. "Generality of an Organizational Commitment Model." *Academy of Management Journal,* 1985, 24: 512–526.

Morris, J. H., and Sherman, J. D. "Generality of an Organizational Commitment Model." *Academy of Management Journal,* 1981, 24: 512–526.

Morris, J. H., and Steers, R. M. "Structural Influences on Organizational Commitment." *Journal of Vocational Behavior,* 1980, 17: 50–57.

Mowday, R. T., Porter, L. W., and Dubin, R. "Unit Performance, Situational Factors, and Employee Attitudes in Spatially Separated Work Units." *Organizational Behavior and Human Performance,* 1974, 12: 231–248.

Mowday, R. T., Steers, R. M., and Porter, L. W. "The Measurement of Organizational Commitment." *Journal of Vocational Behavior,* 1979, 14: 224–247.

Naisbitt, J., and Aburdene, P. *Megatrends 2000.* New York: William Morrow, 1990.

Nanus, B. *The Leader's Edge.* Chicago: Contemporary Books, 1989.

Pava, C. *Managing New Office Technology.* New York: Free Press, 1983.

Pirsig, R. M. *Zen and the Art of Motorcycle Maintenance.* New York: Morrow & Co., 1974.

Peters, T. *Thriving on Chaos.* New York: Alfred A. Knopf, 1988.

Peters, T. J., and Waterman, R. H. *In Search of Excellence.* New York: Harper & Row, 1982.

Proctor, B. H. "A Sociotechnical Work-Design System at Digital Enfield: Utilizing Untapped Resources." *National Productivity Review,* Summer 1986: 262–270.

Randall, D. M. "Commitment and the Organization: The Organization Man Revisited." *Academy of Management Review,* 1987, 12: 460–471.

Reichers, A. E. "A Review and Reconceptualization of Organizational Commitment." *Academy of Management Review,* 1985, 10: 465–476.

Roethlisberger, F., and Dickson, W. *Management and the Worker.* Cambridge, Mass.: Harvard University Press, 1939.

Rosener, J. B. "Ways Women Lead." *Harvard Business Review,* November–December 1990: 119–125.

Scholl, R. W. "Differentiating Organizational Commitment from Expectancy as a Motivating Force." *Academy of Management Review,* 1981, 6: 589–599.

Scott, W. G., and Hart, D. K. *Organizational America.* Boston: Houghton Mifflin, 1981.

Sheldon, M. E. "Investments and Involvements as Mechanisms Producing Commitment to the Organization." *Administrative Science Quarterly,* 1971, 16: 142–150.

Sherwood, J., and Glidewell, J. "Planned Renegotiation: A Norm-Setting OD Intervention." In *Contemporary Organization Development.* Edited by W. W. Burke, La Jolla, Calif.: NTL Learning Resources, 1972.

Steele, F., and Jenks, R. S. *The Feel of the Work Place.* Reading, Mass.: Addison-Wesley, 1977.

Steele, F. *Physical Settings and Organization Development.* Reading, Mass.: Addison-Wesley, 1973.

———, *The Open Organization.* Reading, Mass.: Addison-Wesley, 1975.

Steers, R. "Antecedents and Outcomes of Organizational Commitment." *Adminis-*

trative Science Quarterly, 1977, 22: 46–56.

Steers, R., and Porter, L. "The Role of Task Goal Attributes in Employee Perform-ance." *Psychological Bulletin,* 1974, 81: 434–452.

——, "Employee Commitment to Organizations." In *Motivation and Work Behavior.* Edited by R. Steers and L. Porter, New York: McGraw-Hill, 1983.

Stevens, J. M., Beyer, J. M., and Trice, H. M. "Assessing Personal, Role and Organ-izational Predictors of Managerial Commitment." *Academy of Management Review,* 1978, 21: 380–396.

Taylor, F. W. *The Principles of Scientific Management.* New York: Harper & Row, 1915.

Trist, E. L., and Bamforth, K. W. "Some Social and Psychological Consequences of the Longwall Method of Coal Getting." *Human Relations,* 1951, 4: 3–38.

Vaill, P. *Managing as a Performing Art.* San Francisco: Jossey-Bass, 1989.

Walton, M. *The Deming Method.* New York: Pedigree, 1986.

Walton, R. E. "From Control to Commitment in the Workplace." *Harvard Business Review,* March–April 1985: 77–84.

Weckler, D. A., and Lawrence, A. T. "Creating High-Commitment Organizations through Recruitment and Selection." *The Human Resources Professional,* Spring 1991: 37–43.

Weisbord, M. R. *Productive Workplaces.* San Francisco: Jossey-Bass, 1987.

Whyte, G. "Escalating Commitment to a Course of Action: A Reinterpretation." *Academy of Management Review,* 1986, 11: 311–321.

Wiener, Y. "Commitment in Organizations: A Normative View." *Academy of Management Review,* 1982, 7: 418–428.

Index

About the Author

STEPHEN L. FINK is Professor of Management at the Whittemore School of Business and Economics at the University of New Hampshire in Durham, NH. In addition to his research and teaching, Dr. Fink consults to corporations and is the author of articles and textbooks in organizational behavior and management.